The Business of Negotiation

The Business of Negotiation

An Executive's Guide to Getting What You Want

by Craig A. McKnight, JD

Probabilistic Publishing

Associate Editor: Jeanne Ryan
Associate Editor: Nancy Winchester

Initial printing: December, 2018

Probabilistic Publishing
1702 Hodge Lake Ln
Sugar Land, TX 77478
281-277-4006

www.decisions-books.com
e-mail: dave@decisions-books.com

Written, designed, and printed in the United States of America.

Library of Congress Control Number: 2018965789

ISBN 13: 978-1-941075-04-3
ISBN 10: 1-941075-04-5

To my wife Ginger who put up with me for all these years

Preface

What started me on the path to teaching negotiations and to writing this book on negotiations was simple. I was working with people who *thought* they could negotiate. However, they were giving away the cargo, ship, boat, and dock in their negotiations. They did not even know it. I am sure these people are much better at negotiations now. Well, some of them became better negotiators, I suspect, though trial and many errors.

In business, the first negotiation course I attended was run by Karrass Seminars many years ago. It was an excellent experience. I had the chance to negotiate in class against an excellent negotiator. We deadlocked in our negotiations, which taught me how to get to disagreement but not to come to agreement. Learning how to get to agreement would come a few years later. The class left me with three books to read, but my favorite title of those books is *In Business as in Life – You Don't Get What You Deserve, You Get What You Negotiate*.[1] This book started me on my journey in negotiations. Its title became one of my favorite sayings. I do not know how many times I have said, "You don't get what you deserve; you get what you negotiate."

I purchased the Chester L. Karrass and Zig Zigler negotiation cassette tapes. This was many years ago. I used to listen to the tapes in my car to and from work in Houston's (not-so-lovely) traffic. I love those tapes and the stories, especially by Zig Zigler. Zig told some great negotiation stories.

In October 2000, Chevron bought my employer, Texaco. My new role in Chevron taught me many project management skills, which was very different than my role in Texaco. I found that these project management skills fit very well with managing negotiations. Over the next couple of years, I learned commercial project management. Ultimately, I started teaching project management skills and learned that I loved teaching.

Within two years of the acquisition of Texaco by Chevron, my business unit was put up for sale. I ended up as the commercial project manager for the sale of a technology business and a processing plant. My focus was to sell the businesses and eliminate my position with the company. This was a strange position to be in (but

---

1   Karrass, Chester L., *In Business As in Life, You Don't Get What You Deserve, You Get What You Negotiate*, Stanford Street Press (1996).

not unusual). However, I was somewhat confident my team would find some role in Chevron in the future.

Besides being the commercial project manager for the sale of the assets, I had other duties, including negotiating ancillary contracts for the sale of the assets. After selling the technology business and the processing plant assets, my team received the Chevron Chairman's award for our outstanding performance. We must have done something right after all!

During these asset sales (and in my prior roles), I worked very closely with a fantastic intellectual property lawyer, Morris Reinisch. He introduced me to Jim Thomas' book, *Negotiate to Win, The 21 Rules for Successful Negotiating.*[2] After reading Jim's book, I found my passion: negotiations. Jim's book is easy to read. I highly recommend it. I have read many books on negotiation and related material to expand my knowledge of the practice. Jim's book was by far the best negotiation book as it related to practical advice regarding negotiations.

I almost decided not to write this book after talking to Jim Thomas. Jim told me it took him ten years to write his book. I thought, "That will not happen to me." I suspect many people start to write and quit after they find out how difficult it is to put two sentences together.

After sale of the technology and processing plant assets, I moved to the International Gas Group. In this new job, I was responsible for decision analysis, economic analysis, and commercial processes. I was also responsible for managing various commercial employee networks. I set up employee networks to connect employees from the various business units around the world who were involved in negotiations. This is where I met many more commercial negotiators. I also joined the external group, the International Association of Petroleum Negotiators.

I could see that we at Chevron needed our own "commercial" negotiation course. There were a few externally provided courses over the years but these were too generic in my opinion.

We started to develop the negotiation course over the next year. Once we had a draft, I also facilitated numerous sessions with senior negotiators to review and give feedback on the course. After developing the main course, I found that there was a missing piece in the course – I had not engaged the legal team to get their

---

2   Thomas, Jim, *Negotiate to Win: The 21 Rules for Successful Negotiating*, Harper Business (2005).

feedback. When I worked with the team to sell the technology and processing plant assets, I became fast friends with one of our best lawyers. I worked with him to develop the excellent legal sections of the course.

The ultimate course we developed highlighted examples of missteps and practice sessions with experienced coaches. The course focused on learning from our mistakes, not blame. I rarely told my students who made the mistakes in the negotiation stories (except if it was me).

My students and colleagues have also shared negotiation stories from their own experiences, either asking for advice or just sharing a positive or negative experience with my classes.

I have shared some of these stories in this book. The names have been changed to protect the guilty and the innocent.

The first negotiation course was deployed with great fanfare. We had a hit on our hands. However, I was the only internal teacher of negotiations in a company of 60,000 employees and many more contractors.

At this point, we started traveling all over the world to teach Chevron employees. At the same time, my group provided consulting services to the business units throughout Chevron. It was an excellent networking opportunity for the International Gas Group to engage the company to help with commercial negotiations worldwide.

I collected and implemented the course feedback after teaching many oil and gas professionals from various professions over the next decade. The first class was in Houston. Subsequently, I taught a number of courses in California, Louisiana, Texas, Nigeria, London, Scotland, Australia, Philippines, Singapore, China, and Indonesia. My passion for teaching negotiations was well known throughout the company. I was a requested, regular teacher over and over again in many of these locations. I was also sought out for advice on negotiations worldwide. If I did not have the answer, I would refer employees to other senior company negotiators for help.

These days, I am semi-retired from the business world. I mentor others on decision analysis, negotiations, finance, and whatever comes up. I plan to teach negotiations again but only part-time.

Please note that it is impossible to make the negotiation process exciting. I suspect that is why I could not find the negotiation process in any of the negotiation books I have read. The negotiation books generally focus on tactics and rules. I do address negotiation tactics and rules (including many stories) after discussing the negotiation process. However, you must read and understand the negotiation process first and I have added a few stories to make it interesting. Understanding the negotiation process for business will give you a better understanding of how to implement your negotiation strategies.

Retirement did give me a chance to write this book. If you have any interest in negotiations, I believe you will enjoy reading this book. This is the story of my travels in the business negotiation world, with many lessons that I have learned along the way. I share my experiences so that you may not make some of the mistakes I (and others) have made. You will also find useful tools and tactics that will make your journey in life more successful.

Good luck on your negotiation journey!

Cheers,
Craig A. McKnight, JD
November, 2018

Acknowledgements

This book is a product of many years teaching and working with many knowledgeable people. The people that most helped me understand negotiation over the years are Morris Reinisch, my students, and, most especially, Yao Apasu.

The people that had a significant positive impact on my work and career include Roy Eggenberger, John Van Zant, Joe Gregory, Lee Jourdan, Patsy Nice, Bill McAuley, Mike Illanne, Bevin Wirzba, Brian Putt, Larry Neal, Doug Bartholomew, Doug Quillen, Yao Apasu, Morris Reinisch, Iain Case, John Gass, Byron Wong, Lana Billeaud, Doug Wharton, Jim Houck, Pat Blough, Steve Snider, Steve Wright, and Katrina Kaufman. Thank you all for your candid feedback and interactions during my career.

We really appreciate the candid feedback from Doug Quillen, Yao Apasu, Larry Neal, Brian Putt, and my wife, Ginger on this book. Also, thank you Nancy Winchester and Jeanne Ryan for your excellent editing work!

Disclaimer

Notwithstanding the affiliation of the writer, or anything contained herein or in the communication hereof to the contrary, this book and any statement made, or material issued, by the writer in connection herewith represent the sole and independent position of the writer and do not necessarily reflect the position of any of the writer's prior employers or their affiliates.

The information contained herein is for general guidance only. The application and impact of laws can vary widely depending on the facts and circumstances. The author is not rendering legal, accounting, tax, or other professional advice. The information herein should not be used as a substitute for consultation with professional accounting, tax, legal or other competent advisors.

Note: I include this disclaimer in some form in all my presentations and thought it should go in this book... You have to figure out what works for you; this book is no exception. Caveat Emptor!

Contents

Story Titles

1
Objectives and Contracts

Negotiation books include rules and tactics, but they do not provide the *process* of negotiations. Maybe professors and other writers think the process is intuitive, but my experience has proven otherwise.

I spent much of the last 20 years of my career researching and working to develop negotiation processes and tools. These processes and tools have helped many individuals and project teams get what they wanted, not just what they needed.

While I have great respect for negotiation book writers and even recommend some of their books, these writers missed a great opportunity to explain what we should be doing to prepare for any negotiation. The most important part of negotiation is doing your homework prior to ever interacting with your counterparty. There is a *process* that should be followed, even for simple negotiations. The process may be shortened to fit your needs, depending on the complexity of the negotiation.

It is my job with this book to explain the negotiation process. I will share the key negotiation rules and tactics as clearly and in as few words as possible. I will also share many stories along the way. You may forget a rule or tactic, but you rarely forget the corresponding stories.

Before I developed the Chevron internal negotiation course, we only hired external negotiation providers for Chevron employees. These courses focused on rules, tactics, and short generic practice exercises, but not the negotiation process. One of the reasons I am writing this book is to provide the negotiation process.

The Panicked Team

During the first internal negotiation class I taught for Chevron, I really did not understand the nature of the teams. I had randomly established the negotiating teams for the course. One of the teams approached me at the end of the first day to tell me they were absolutely lost. They did not understand the main negotiation example. They were "scared" to take on their counterparty in the scheduled negotiations practice sessions for day two of the course.

This team consisted of very junior employees. Their counterparty was a much more experienced team and face-to-face negotiations started fairly early on day two. The junior team told me they did not understand the terms and conditions set forth in the main example. The terms to be negotiated included price, volumes, liquidated damage provisions, and a few other issues. I recognized that I needed to educate them better on the negotiation example on day one (but this was hindsight at this point). I had assigned coaches to each team for day two (but not day one).

My motto in teaching is that you learn much more from your failures than from your successes. If you are one of my former students, please know that it was and is OK to make mistakes in my class. My main objective is for my students not to repeat the same mistakes in real life negotiations.

Day two came and went quickly (as it always does in a two-day negotiation course). The junior team came to me after the second day. They told me they felt they were now better negotiators. The experience they had was a lot of fun. They truly believed they could take on anyone at that point. The coaches helped them understand the terms and conditions better in order to negotiate.

Taking any negotiation course instills some confidence, but does not necessarily make you competent. Experience is the best teacher, but experience can be a cruel master when you get hammered in a negotiation class and, more importantly, in real life.

Generally, your coach, on any subject that you need to understand, is your subject matter expert (SME). Many times, you, as the negotiator, will negotiate an issue with your counterparty, not your SME. You need to understand the issue in great detail in order to negotiate for the SME. This requires you to interview the SME and learn all you can on the subject.

Just to reemphasize the need for practice, I have always asked my students and kids if they knew what it takes to get to Carnegie Hall. (The younger folks have no idea what I am talking about.) However, the correct answer is *practice, practice, practice.* The memory is weak; you must practice what you learn. Generally, you will lose most of what you learn within a short period of time. Negotiation is not like riding a bike; you will get lazy or complacent without practice. Also, please do not attempt to practice negotiations on your spouse if you want to stay married...

After reading this book, you should understand the following:

1. The *negotiation process* from beginning to end, including exposure to useful tools that will help you get alignment along the way.

2. The key negotiation rules and tactics used for business and in life.

3. The most important part of negotiation is doing your homework.

4. You need to adapt to situations, depending on the nature of your negotiations.

5. You will need to pick two to three tactics that you think you are good at and practice them.

6. If you break a negotiation rule, you must be prepared to suffer the consequences or attempt to mitigate the impact.

The key rules and tactics in this book are what I have come to understand through many years of study, teaching, and practice. They are not meant to be all inclusive or have all the answers to every question you have. In fact, I suggest you develop in your own words a set of negotiation processes, rules and tactics applicable to your negotiations even if they are very similar to mine. I believe this is the only way to reinforce the use of the most important processes, rules or tactics.

Before we talk about the negotiation process, let us discuss different types of agreements and contracts.

Different Types of Contracts

The following is meant to give you an understanding of the different types of contracts. It is not meant to be all inclusive nor is it legal advice. You need a good team that includes competent tax and legal professionals to assist you along the way with your contracts.

Commercial contracts can cover a variety of non-technical and technical issues, including pricing, volumes, damages, responsibilities of the parties, and specifications. A contract, also known as an agreement, is any legally enforceable promise between parties. A contract may be in writing but can be oral, depending on the circumstances. Contracts should align parties on each party's rights and obligations during the term of the contract.

Contracts are generally formal documents in the project world but may be found on invoices, letters, and proposals. When writing any contract, the duration of the investment and potential future events need to be taken into consideration.

Public and many non-public companies generally require contracts to be authorized, written, and approved by formally designated individuals within the organization. These companies have *delegations of authority* to identify the approving managers.

Some agreements may be negotiated long before project agreements are negotiated, such as concession agreements with governments. A *concession agreement* allows the holder to operate in some form in country during the term of the agreement. The project teams must understand these agreements and any effect these signed agreements will have on future contracts being negotiated. Some impacts include budget, schedule, scope, the project execution plan, government approvals, and project economics. Some examples of agreements are:

- Shareholder,
- Joint development,
- Supplier,
- Vendor,
- Sales and purchase,
- Joint operating,
- Host government,
- Concession,
- Production sharing,
- Service, and
- Transportation.

Every project is unique. The project team must understand how all the agreements affect the project and when these agreements should be developed.

Different Types of Intermediate Agreements

Depending on the complexity of the transaction being negotiated, an agreement may go through a number of intermediate development steps before it is concluded to a Comprehensive Binding Agreement, such as:

1. Memorandum of Understanding (MOU),

2. Letter of Intent (LOI), and

3. Heads of Agreement (HOA).

These agreements are further defined in the following paragraphs.

    A *Memorandum of Understanding* (MOU) is a basic co-operation agreement that describes the terms the parties will work together prior to having a more formal agreement. An

MOU generally has limited binding effect and could include public announcements, confidentiality, termination, scope, preliminary technical work, timing, cost sharing, and intellectual property.

A *Letter of Intent* (LOI) is similar to an MOU but may have more binding effect. An LOI may also include management structure (names, charter, procedures), funding, support, governing law, exclusivity, rights of refusal, conflict of interest, and decision-making protocols. Following the negotiation of the LOI, due diligence should be performed (since the parties are stating their intent to do something).

A *Heads of Agreement* (HOA) is similar to a LOI or MOU, but the parties further agree on binding terms and is a more comprehensive agreement.

Comprehensive Binding Agreements form the legal and commercial foundation of the transaction. Comprehensive agreements are generally needed prior to project approval. Until final, this form of agreement may be considered some form of the above agreements since issues may continue to come up to be addressed.

Comprehensive Binding Agreements may be developed with similar or different terms than in the MOU, LOI, or HOA previously negotiated.

Warnings!

All of these agreements should be carefully reviewed and approved by your key subject matter experts, including your lawyer and tax counsel. Additionally, the Lead Negotiator is ultimately responsible for all content in these documents and should ask for help for any area not well understood and look for inconsistencies between the documents.

Almost all companies have some type of acceptance or ratification process when the document is not within the approval authority of the person negotiating the agreement. It is very important that you early on understand your and your counterparty's process to get your contracts approved.

It is usually in your best interest to help your counter-party with selling the decision internally in their company, especially if it is a difficult sell.

Do not forget this step since it will come back to bite you when your counterparty takes forever to get something approved internally. Additionally, subject matter experts and executives may start to criticize your agreement if they are not kept informed. It is up to you to have a good communication plan with subject matter experts and management.

I also hope this book encourages you to go practice negotiations and even take a negotiation course.

Questions

1. What are the objectives of this book?

2. What is a Memorandum of Understanding?

3. What is a Letter of Intent?

4. What is a Heads of Agreement?

5. When is a Comprehensive Binding Agreement an intermediate agreement?

6. Why is it important to determine the type of agreement to be negotiated early in a negotiation?

2
The Negotiation Process

This chapter discusses the complete negotiation process. Note that *practice* will inherently give you a much better understanding of this process.

Learning the negotiation process is a *must* for anyone who wants to be good negotiator. There is much more to negotiating than simply engaging the counterparty.

The stages of the negotiation process are:

1. Assess the opportunity (Chapter 3),

2. Develop a team and organization structure (Chapter 4),

3. Gather information (Chapter 5),

4. Develop negotiation positions and strategies (Chapter 6),

5. Negotiate externally (Chapter 7), and

6. Close and Plan the transition (Chapter 8).

These negotiation processes generally overlap and are not necessarily sequential. You may also need to recycle between stages.

Recycle might include the need to discover additional information during meetings with your counterparty to determine a negotiation strategy on an issue. Another example would be (and this has happened to me many times), you discover something during the face-to-face negotiations that you thought you knew. Surprises will happen and may even shock you. Count on surprises and adapt.

I was asked to assist with negotiating several agreements with a national oil company (NOC) many years ago. When I engaged, it was unclear who our Lead Negotiator was. I found out that our company had *several* Lead Negotiators in the past. I also found out the parties had been negotiating the agreements for a couple of years. The relationship with the NOC was not good and the contracts were not even in draft writing at that point. Recycle was a necessity to get organized.

All of these processes will be explained in more detail in later chapters. However, here is an overview of each stage of the negotiation process.

(1) Assess the Opportunity

The first part of the process is assessing the opportunity. This is *framing* the negotiation. Framing is a process I rarely see in negotiations but it is the correct place to start. Framing creates the dialog to get the overall team aligned and focused on the opportunity: what success looks like, value drivers, issues, assumptions, facts, decisions, and action items.

The Last-Minute General Manager

I was facilitating preparation for complex negotiations. I kept asking the General Manager to see the framing document prior to the session and provided a template. Fortunately, on the day of the first meeting, the General Manager provided a pre-frame. We used his pre-frame as a guide. We were able to complete the frame and get better alignment. Over the next three days, we developed the action plans and information for these negotiations. There were around 18 people in the negotiation planning meeting. Preparation is a necessity to avoid wasting time, especially when you have a larger group to facilitate.

(2) Develop a Team and Organization Structure

The second part of the process is developing the overall team and setting up the organizational structure. The negotiating team participates in the negotiations on a regular basis and may consist of a lead negotiator, a second chair, a lawyer and an analyst. This requires understanding the type of negotiation, the dollar value of the negotiation and competencies required. In addition to the negotiating team, you will need subject matter experts (SMEs).

You will need the negotiating team plus others to help develop the framing document. Since the negotiating team does not have all the answers, some subject matter experts will need to be engaged to help fill in the blanks. Depending on the nature of your negotiation, you may have a fully dedicated team or a part-time team. To the extent you can get your requirements on performance agreements of your negotiating team and the subject matter experts, you will be more likely to get their time.

When the President Calls

On one occasion, I was asked to explain why the economics of a project that was being built was deteriorating. I was told by a Vice President to take someone on my team that was part of a lot of the potential problems. I was happy with the negotiating team at this point.

I remember telling the Vice President that I had a good team and did not want him on my team. Fortunately, it was the President of the company that called to ask me to find out what was going on with the project. I suspect my conversation with the Vice President may have been career limiting at the time. In hindsight, I offered later to have him as a subject matter expert, which worked. Sometimes you have to save yourself.

It is important to get the right people on your team at the right time and maintain good relationships.

(3) Gather Information

The third part of the process is gathering information that will be needed to generate your contract positions before and during the negotiations. This can include whom you are negotiating with, any available publicly available information and any of the information available on the subject matter internally.

However, you will not have all the information you think you need going into a negotiation. Some information just may not be available, such as potential damages. You may have to estimate these costs in the contract. You will find out more information in discussions with your counterparty, which will necessitate changing your negotiations positions. You may be surprised that information you thought you knew is wrong. It is important to check all information you receive from your counterparty if possible.

A Lack of Reference

Just to give you something that should never happen, I remember negotiating a contract for sale of product to a third party. I was helping facilitate the negotiation planning as we were negotiating with our counterparty. Our lawyers had added a reference to a separate agreement that I had never seen before. I asked the lawyer whether he thought the agreement was material and why I had not seen the agreement before.

I was a little upset as you might imagine. Planning will help with action items to hold people accountable to get the information you need. Sometimes things do get overlooked but please make this the exception not the rule in your negotiations.

Information is power. The better prepared you are, the more likely your outcomes will be favorable.

(4) Develop Negotiation Positions and Strategies

The fourth part of the process is developing and maintaining your and your counterparty's negotiation strategies and contract position of each issue. This is a critical part of successful negotiations. Besides understanding your wants, needs, and must haves in the contract, you need to try to understand your counterparty's wants, needs, and must haves.

Unfortunately, we cannot gaze into a crystal ball to see what our counterparty is thinking. During this process of trying to understand what your counterparty will want, put yourself in the counterparty's position in the negotiation. Ask yourself, "What would I want, what would I need and what must I have?"

You can then develop a negotiation strategy, but it will probably have gaps unless you really understand what your counterparty wants. This is an evolving process as more and more information becomes available.

When Economics Don't Matter

I remember walking into a meeting where the team was developing a strategy to move a project forward. They were weighting and ranking the issues as they went through the process. However, there was an extremely important issue that the facilitator ignored: the economics. I walked into the meeting to interrupt the flow of discussion. I asked the team why they would want to do this project with such poor economics. I did not get an answer and they proceeded.

I found out later that upper management had decided that this project needed to done regardless of how bad the economics were. When something like this happens, you really need to be prepared to try to mitigate the damage. I do have some examples later on in the book that actually have good outcomes due to preparation and good leadership.

You are really never through with this process until you finish the negotiations. This process should include negotiating internally inside your company and with your consultants. Most people do not understand that internal discussions are negotiations, especially those with management. You must be prepared for each of these interactions.

(5) Negotiate Externally

The fifth part of the process is engaging your counterparty in negotiations.

On most project negotiations, the first meeting should be focused on meeting the counterparty, sharing scripted or plan information and getting as much information out of your counterparty as possible. You may need several of these type meetings before either of you are prepared to start discussing the agreement in any detail.

Later meetings should be set to start the contract negotiations with your counterparty to discuss:

- The type of agreement to be negotiated (e.g., term sheet),
- Whom you are meeting with,
- What the issues are to be discussed,
- Timing constraints associated with the issues, and
- Who is your counterparty's decision maker during each of the negotiations meetings?

I have attended various difficult negotiation meetings, such as:

- The counterparty's lead negotiator did not show up for a week of scheduled meetings,
- The counterparty addressed issues we did not agree to discuss nor were we prepared to discuss,
- The counterparty was not prepared to discuss the issues that we agreed to discuss,
- The wrong people attended, limiting any chance of get anything done,
- We had to tell the counterparty that we could not keep a prior promise made by management (and that executive was at that meeting), and
- When a material difficult issue came up early in a meeting, killing any chance of making any progress for weeks.

Do not take missteps personally, it is business and sometimes plays into their strategy. It can get frustrating at times though.

As you find out more information during your interactions with your counterparty, you will need to continue to update your negotiation strategy and prepare for the next interaction. You should have determined you own approval processes and deadlines during your information gathering process. Your deadlines may change; please keep your deadlines updated to avoid surprises.

You will need to find out from your counterparty any deadlines and approval processes at some point during your discussions. If you ask too early, you may not get a good answer. If you ask too late, you may get surprised.

(6) Close and Plan the Transition

The sixth part of the process is closing the deal and transition planning.

When selling assets, closing may include negotiating not only the main asset sale but also subsequently negotiating various transition type agreements.

The Sub-Negotiation

In one transaction I was working, we closed on the main contract but we still had to complete another eight ancillary contracts prior to closing. Deadlines were fast approaching. We handled all these ancillary agreements as a separate project including developing a schedule, keeping action items, having regular meetings to determine status and progressing all the contracts together in order to meet the deadline.

Generally, your negotiators will not transition with the contract to operations. Some other person in the company will probably handle the operations, implementation of that contract, and transition of any assets. It is important to make the transition as seamless as possible to move the people and assets into the buyer from the seller to avoid more disruptions. As we know, change is already a disrupter.

Questions

1. What are the stages of the negotiation process?

2. Why would you use framing in the negotiation process?

3. Why are negotiations not linear?

4. When developing your negotiating strategy on an issue, what are the three pieces of information you need to develop?

5. Why would you need to recycle your thinking around your position on an issue?

6. What personal experiences have you had in negotiations when you had a good outcome? Why?

7. What personal experiences have you had in negotia-
    tions when you had a bad outcome? Why?

8. Why would you need to understand who you are meet-
    ing with in a negotiation session?

9. Why would you need to plan what issues you are going
    to discuss in a meeting?

3
Assess the Opportunity

In this chapter, we will discuss framing, which is part of the focus of Decision Analysis (DA). Decision Analysis is the overall activity of framing and analysis, which is designed to improve team discussions, to get clarity of action, and to enable better decisions. While you may not need to do a lot of analytics to support your negotiations, it makes sense to understand the frame of your negotiations. This will get alignment of your team and create actions plans about your and your counterparty contract positions. If you want to know more about the analytical side of Decision Analysis, I suggest *Introduction to Decision Analysis*, 3rd Edition,[3] *Why Can't You Just Give Me The Number?* 2nd Edition,[4] and *Decision Analysis for Managers*, 2nd Edition.[5] My focus in this book is on framing your negotiation.

Decision Analysis is all about getting good decision quality. To do that, you need alignment on your objectives, risks, and uncertainties. Framing fits well with negotiation, since you need your negotiating team, your non-core team, and the decision maker aligned on where you are going to take the negotiations. The decision maker may be your manager, an executive, the business owner, or even the board of directors. Generally, the decision maker makes or approves the key

---

3   Skinner, David C., *Introduction to Decision Analysis*, 3rd Edition, Probabilistic Publishing (2009).

4   Leach, Patrick, *Why Can't You Just Give Me The Number?*, 2nd Edition, Probabilistic Publishing (2014).

5   Charlesworth, David, *Decision Analysis for Managers*, 2nd Edition, Business Expert Press (2017).

company impactful decisions regarding the agreement. The negotiating team tends to make most of the contract decisions during the negotiations.

I have also included a framing template as an Appendix to this book for you to use. Use this framing template to prepare for any negotiation. The framing template is mostly self-explanatory, but here are some key points to consider.

The parts of a frame are very well defined and include the following:

1. Problem (or Opportunity) Statement[6]

This is focused on understanding what the problem, risk, or opportunity is and why you are trying to solve it. Many people want to solve the problem during this initial process. This is malpractice in framing. How to solve the problem will come later as you do more homework and you meet with your counterparty. At this point, you have more questions than answers, but you have to start here.

2. Boundary Conditions

The focus here is understanding what issues are within, outside of, or on the frame.

Outside of the frame are those issues that your contract will not address for various reasons. It may be that they are addressed in a separate contract or are handled elsewhere.

Documenting the issues in the frame helps get the negotiating team to focus on the issues that need to be handled.

If the issue is on the frame, you are uncertain whether you need to negotiate it or not at the time you put the original frame together. You need to determine if the decision maker wants your negotiating team to negotiate these issues. Those issues listed as inside the frame should be high level in boundary conditions since the issue raising section of the

---

6   For a discussion on the differences in approach between problems, risks, and opportunities (and management's biases relative to each), see *Decision Analysis for Managers*, 2nd Edition, by David Charlesworth. For a more thorough discussion, see *Problem, Risk, and Opportunity Enterprise Management* by Brian Hagen.

frame should bring the detail you need later in the framing session.

3. What is Success?

Here you need to think about what the decision maker really wants, when does he or she want it, and how much he or she wants to spend to get it. Later discussions with the decision maker after the framing session will help clarify what success will look like. Your decision maker generally should not be in your framing session.

4. Issues

This is a brainstorming session looking for facts, assumptions, decisions, uncertainties, risks, decision metrics, and other issues.

5. Objectives Hierarchy

This includes what your team wants relative to the problem, risk, or opportunity and notes tradeoffs between objectives. This is an elaboration of the "What is Success?" step.

6. Decision Time Line

Once you have listed your decisions in the issue raising, you need to determine which are:

- ♦ Given decisions (decisions that have already been made),
- ♦ Strategic or focus decisions (decisions that need to be made now), and
- ♦ Tactical (later) decisions.

Your focus decisions are what you need to do now to complete your current actions items. Later focus decisions do not need to be handled now but are documented for later handling. Putting these decisions on a time line can help the team understand and reach alignment on how the negotiations are likely to progress.

7. SWOT Analysis

Strengths, weaknesses, opportunities, and threats may be listed to better understand internal strengths and weaknesses and external opportunities and threats.

8. Key Stakeholders Analysis

Understanding who are impacted internally and externally, including government entities, is important. Since most of what you are dealing with is confidential, you must develop a communication plan, including keeping your decision maker informed.

9. Action Items

Action items need to be developed and maintained to determine what are next steps after each meeting. The negotiating team should have regularly scheduled meetings to update action items, to make sure activities are completed timely, and to plan for upcoming events.

Framing

There are a lot of good resources to get information on framing outside of this book, but I wanted to give you a flavor of framing. You should revisit the frame periodically to see if you missed something.

Framing your negotiation will help you achieve better results and get alignment of your teams and management. Unless your negotiation is very complicated, this activity should not take long. Pre-work the frame in a small subset of the team if you will have a large number of people in your framing session.

More complicated negotiations should take the necessary time and not short cut this. Benjamin Franklin is credited with the saying, "If you fail to plan, you are planning to fail." I agree completely.

Questions

1. What are the two characteristics of an Problem or an Opportunity Statement?

2. What should you avoid discussing when developing the opportunity statement?

3. What is the purpose of Decision Analysis?

4. What are boundary conditions and why would you want to establish them?

5. Why would you want to develop what a successful negotiation outcome would be?

6. What are the main types of decisions in a negotiation? Why would you separate the decision into each grouping?

7. Why would you want to understand agendas of key stakeholders?

8. Why would you want to revisit the frame periodically?

9. What are the key parts of an action plan? Why would you need to maintain and update action plans?

4

Team and Organizational Structure

Developing your team and getting organized is an important part of your negotiation process. As you develop the frame, you need to build your team. You may also find that during the framing session you are missing critical members to add to your team. You may also find that later in the negotiation others will need to be included who had not been considered previously.

Business negotiations are often complex and time-consuming and require significant commitment of resources, including subject matter experts (SMEs). Your contract negotiations might be part of a much larger project that has an overall project manager. Commercial issues are generally not well understood by project managers (who also tend to be schedule driven). Project managers generally want to know when you are going to sign and complete the contract on their project. If your contract is on the critical path of a project, the project manager may be a frequent visitor to your meetings and to your office.

To help identify the scale and magnitude of activities, Figure 4.1 shows the team organizational chart for your negotiations for more complex business transactions.

The typical negotiating team in a commercial negotiation includes a Lead Negotiator, a Second Chair, a Lawyer, and an Analyst. The SMEs are considered part of the extended or non-core team. However, there might be a need to change the structure depending on the circumstances. Additionally, in some cases, the lawyer may be the Lead Negotiator, especially for confidentiality agreements, intellectual property, and vendor-type contracts.

Let's explore each key role of the negotiating team.

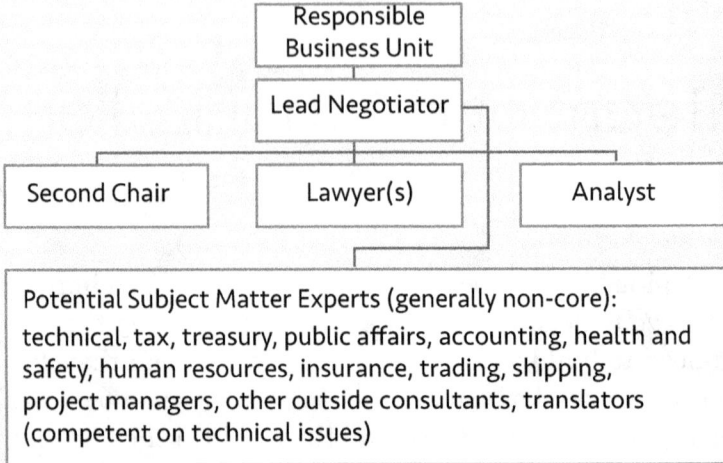

```
            ┌─────────────────────┐
            │    Responsible      │
            │   Business Unit     │
            └─────────────────────┘
            ┌─────────────────────┐
            │   Lead Negotiator   │──┐
            └─────────────────────┘
┌──────────────┐  ┌──────────────┐  ┌──────────────┐
│ Second Chair │  │  Lawyer(s)   │  │   Analyst    │
└──────────────┘  └──────────────┘  └──────────────┘
```

Potential Subject Matter Experts (generally non-core): technical, tax, treasury, public affairs, accounting, health and safety, human resources, insurance, trading, shipping, project managers, other outside consultants, translators (competent on technical issues)

Figure 4.1: Recommended Commercial Negotiation Overall Team Structure

Lead Negotiator

The Lead Negotiator is the person on the negotiating team who makes the final team decisions on issues after discussion with the negotiating team. Decisions can also be made by team consensus. This person is the main interface with the counterparty and may be the main interface with the decision maker. The Lead Negotiator is responsible for, or may delegate:

♦ Setting up meetings with counterparties,

♦ Understanding who is going to attend the meetings,

♦ Agreeing what issues should be discussed,

♦ Gets the appropriate parties or SMEs to be at the negotiations, and

♦ Generally does most of the talking during interactions with the counterparty (unless agreed to otherwise).

Sometimes some of these activities are delegated to other parties on the team. In some cultures, delegating these activities is the norm (e.g., Japan).

Second Chair

The Second Chair can take the Lead Negotiator's role if the Lead Negotiator is absent from any meeting (if so agreed with the Lead Negotiator). The Second Chair is also a member of the negotiating team in order to gain experience. In our mobile society, the Second Chair may need to take over the role of the Lead Negotiator. He or she needs the history to be better prepared when the counterparty indicates something has already been agreed that is not. Companies and individuals need to train and pass on knowledge of experienced negotiators to the next generation through experience, not just training. A Second Chair is needed for more complicated negotiations and certainly if the person needs experience.

Analyst

Your Analyst is part of the negotiating team to help to better understand the calculated value of any issue that needs to be negotiated. Your Analyst may or may not directly participate in the face-to-face negotiations. It is up to the Lead Negotiator to determine whether this is necessary. It is much better for the Analyst to receive information promptly or in real time. The Analyst should be available during your internal and external negotiations to allow you to better understand the value of any issue in real time.

Your Analyst generally is the part-time negotiation project manager. The better analysts should be able to assist with facilitation of meetings, decision tools, and framing sessions.

Lawyer

The lawyer plays many roles. These roles include advisor, advocate, negotiator, and legal evaluator depending on the nature of your negotiations.

As an advisor, the lawyer focuses on your company's legal rights and obligations, including identifying legal risks and uncertainties.

As an advocate, the lawyer represents the company in litigation, mediation, and arbitration if necessary.

As a legal evaluator, the lawyer is there to help you navigate company compliance processes, ensure accuracy in memorializing the documents, ensure consistency with other agreements, and to advise the negotiating team on what the agreement actually means if unclear or ambiguous.

As a negotiator, the lawyer focuses on getting the best deal for the company and on ethical deal making. The lawyer's role in negotiations needs to be defined when forming the negotiating team, whether you are using in-house or outside counsel. Some in-house lawyers think they are supposed to make the commercial decisions during the negotiations. The commercial team should rely on the lawyer to give advice on commercial issues since most business lawyers have had substantial experience on various issues. However, the Lead Negotiator is ultimately responsible for the business outcomes and should be given deference on commercial issues unless the decision maker (or the person or persons who will ultimately approve the deal) has indicated otherwise.

The Short-Sighted General Counsel

It seems we continue to learn from our mistakes. We did not understand what was publicly available prior to a negotiation that happened some years ago. There was a contract that was being negotiated with a small publicly held company. The lawyer and the Lead Negotiator on that particular contract were fairly capable individuals. However, they had never negotiated this type of contract before.

They proceeded to negotiate the contracts over several months with the third-party. During that time, I was fortunate enough to have dinner with our company's General Counsel. During dinner that night, I literally got on one knee begged him to hire outside counsel to help in this negotiation because I believed that our negotiating team did not know what it was doing. The General Counsel told me the existing negotiating team could handle the negotiations. Outside counsel was not allowed to be hired for this negotiation. He told me the lawyer had experience in these types of contracts.

Subsequently, the negotiations proceeded and were completed by that negotiating team. The resulting contract is one of the worst contracts I have ever seen. Ironically, the commercial person was blamed for the outcome and the lawyer was promoted.

Additionally, a similar (and better) contract was finalized with this particular counterparty prior to negotiations with the counterparty. This contract was publicly available at the United States Securities and Exchange Commission (SEC) during our negotiations.

To make matters worse, the approving executive did not understand the commercial issues of the contract or related to the industry. The executive just wanted an agreement at "all" costs. This was a recipe for failure.

Subject Matter Experts

Subject matter experts (SMEs) generally are your technical experts and may or may not have a substantial amount of negotiating experience. Therefore, SMEs participation in face-to-face negotiations should be planned ahead of time and limited. When it is of strategic advantage to have SMEs in the room with the counterparty, do so.

It is important to engage SMEs early in the process. Otherwise, they become opponents, not proponents of your contract. As Figure 4.1 shows, there are many kinds of subject matter experts who can be involved in your negotiations. It is imperative that the core team understands what its needs are for the contract to allow time for SMEs to respond timely.

SME information can drive boundaries and trade-offs during the negotiation. In order to do this, the negotiating team must be educated on the needs and wants of each SME. Therefore, it is important that the negotiating team interviews each SME to determine what the SME's needs and wants are, if not addressed otherwise.

There are some instances where an SME-required language is not critical to the contract. The negotiating team must engage the SME to explain the nature of what had to be done to close the contract if their proposed language was not included in the final contract. This is especially true when dealing with corporate departments, since they may undermine your contract negotiations with decision maker(s) or other management. Network within your company early and often; however, you also must be careful with confidential information and sharing too broadly.

In all meetings with counterparties, make sure you brief any SME or manager on their role. Be specific as possible, including what the SME and manager are allowed to say and not to say. There have been a number of instances where SMEs or management were in the negotiations after hard-fought discussions on particular issues. The SME or manager then gave away these issues or too much information to the counterparty, which undermined the negotiating team's progress.

Sometimes the SMEs have a relationship with employees of your counterparty. It is important to make sure your SMEs act in your best interest. You should always ask if they know anyone on the other side. Technical experts seem to have small communities, so you never know unless you ask. However, on the positive side, you might be able to gain additional information that you otherwise would not be able to obtain.

Management and SMEs may have on their annual performance agreements to complete your contract by a certain date, regardless of the value destruction. You may also have a deadline on your own annual performance agreement. You need to be prepared to make a case that the value destruction substantially outweighs completion of the contract if you cannot close the agreement on time. Good luck with this, as I have rarely been successful at convincing management that the agreement needed more time, even when it did. Hence, sometimes, annual performance reviews can be painful.

I want to briefly discuss *needs* versus *wants*. Generally, when we put forth an initial key position in a contract, it represents a *want*. I should have additional room to move off of that want to close the deal or that issue. However, if it is a *need* on a particular issue, it is generally considered to be a requirement. Therefore, we must test whether the *need* is really a bottom line when interviewing the SMEs or is just a *want*. On material items, a need becomes a *must have* and may kill your deal if you cannot find an alternate solution.

Overall Team Management

Now we have gone through the discussion of creating the overall team. You need to understand that managing all resources is very different from managing the negotiating team itself. I listed a number of potential subject matter experts (SME) in Figure 4.1. You may need their time and support in your negotiations. If you can get support from management of your SMEs, then they will dedicate more time to your particular negotiation than other activities. Most SMEs have many masters since they have many work activities in addition to your agreements.

In the framing template, there is a section for maintaining action items. Action items should be maintained throughout the negotiation process to help you keep track of details and data from various internal parties, including your negotiating team and your SMEs. Make the responsible party one of your negotiating team members in the action item list in order to split the duty. This will also limit the number of people in your meetings. You can also have a particular meeting for specific issues affecting specific SMEs. In the comments section of the action item list, you should list who the SMEs are, including any updates.

There are some pitfalls that you might run into when setting up your negotiating team. Picking negotiating teams is inherently risky. Big negotiating teams are hard to control. Information may not remain confidential, or someone may slip up since there are more members of your team open to questions by the other side. Some people are too talkative for their own good. Informal settings with your counterparty (such as cocktails or dinner after a long day) can be disastrous or can be a windfall of great information. Make sure you plan ahead so that your team knows what to do, including seeking additional information.

Keep your negotiating team as small as practical and brief members who are not needed in the negotiations if they attend any meetings with the counterparty.

Use a big team on the other side to your advantage.

Target Rich Territory

For example, I was in a negotiation with my counterparty's large negotiating team. I had my two lawyers at my side. The counterparty had seven people sitting on the other side of the table. A big business issue came up in our contract discussions with their Lead Negotiator, who was also their lead lawyer. We had been negotiating for a number of months at this point. Fortunately, I had developed credibility with their commercial business people.

I decided on this particular issue that I would not talk only to their Lead Negotiator but also to the lead commercial person. After discussing the issue for some time and explaining to their side, their lawyer was continuing to shake his head "NO" the whole time. After a long period of time explaining the issue, their lead commercial person got up out of his chair went to the whiteboard. He started writing down exactly what I was talking about. He even said I was right. This overruled their lawyer and closed on the particular issue.

Strategy is important. Sometimes you need to adjust in the moment to get to agreement instead of staying at disagreement. I have used this approach with confidentiality agreements.

Educated Change

My lawyer negotiated very complicated technology confidentiality agreements when we were selling some assets. I then took over as the commercial lead negotiating these agreements with my counterparty's lawyers. We jointly negotiated at least 35 confidentiality agreements for a technology divestiture. Even though their lawyer disagreed with me, there were several instances where their commercial lead overruled their lawyer. If the negotiation was lawyer-to-lawyer, I am fairly sure the negotiation would have been much more difficult and their commercial lead would have deferred to his own lawyer.

Sometimes it might be in your best interest to change the Lead Negotiator. However, I have seen changing the Lead Negotiator backfire. I have an example of a bad outcome when we changed the Lead Negotiator coming up in the next section on decision makers.

Avoid negotiating price early in your discussions, since risks and damages should be negotiated before the price can be settled. While you may feel uneasy putting time into an agreement without having an idea of price, price is a function of the key terms and risks in the agreement.

I have seen project managers push negotiating teams to address price early.

The Project Manager That Needed Fixing

I remember one time when I was approached by the lead commercial business person for help with her project manager. The team had never met with their counterparty in Africa, but the project manager wanted to quote the most advantageous price to deliver product at their first meeting.

We had to advise the project manager that when he quotes the lowest price they would get at the outset, it sets the negotiation up for failure. The counterparty would probably sell their management on the good price, which the team probably can never achieve. Since the price was at or close to our bottom line, the counterparty would probably want significant reductions in price from the first quoted price.

Ideally, the negotiating team should know throughout the negotiations what is acceptable to management. It should seek management's support, especially on key issues if not already given. Additionally, the negotiating team should do their homework to help management make quality decisions.

Decision Makers

While the negotiating team is generally responsible for the decisions in the negotiation, they still have to answer to executive management or the key decision maker.

Therefore, understanding the approval process and requirements for approvals are an important part of the information gathering process. You need to determine how you are going to seek approval of your agreement. There are many different ways to seek approvals, including:

♦ Obtain a mandate from management on the key terms and conditions to authorize the negotiating team to negotiate the deal. The team may agree on issues as long as it stays within bottom lines of the key terms and conditions provided to management. You need to test the key terms to understand if the key terms are really deal breakers.

♦ Have a single point contact in executive management during the negotiations to seek approval or modification of key terms. There are always trade-offs in any negotiation. Some key terms can be modified if the deal as a whole appears favorable. This requires ongoing briefings with executive management while the negotiation is taking place with the counterparty.

♦ Seek approval of the agreement once all terms and conditions are negotiated. This may be completed as part of a major project or separately for an individual need.

I have seen management and the negotiating team disagree on terms and conditions prior to or during negotiations. This create issues internally, especially when the negotiating team returns with an agreement that management believes is subpar.

A Failure to Communicate

For instance, I know a negotiator that I would rank as one of the best negotiators in the processing industry. This is due in part to her experience level in the processing industry, including having run a processing plant in the 1980's, which is quite remarkable in the oil and gas industry.

She was asked by her manager to negotiate a processing agreement with a plant owner that had a monopoly in the area where her company was producing natural gas and liquids. She knew the owner fairly well since she had worked in the industry for a number of years. She prepared and negotiated the final terms and conditions directly with the owner of the processing facility. This took several months of negotiations. She and her boss did not communicate sufficiently about the agreement during the negotiations.

With final agreement in hand, she arrived at the office to show her boss. After briefly reviewing the agreement, her boss told her that the processing fee was too high. He was expecting a much lower fee. Needless to say, this did not go over very well with my friend. The expectation of a lower processing fee was not communicated nor did she ask for his expectations. Also, she was by far the more experienced than her boss in negotiating and understanding processing agreements.

Her boss then told her to get a lower fee from the owner of the processing plant. Her response was, "This is as good as it gets." She was unwilling to negotiate further with the owner of the processing facility. The manager then sent another negotiator to renegotiate terms of the agreement. What do you think happened to him?

The new negotiator went to visit the plant owner and advised him that the processing fee needed to be lower. Upon receiving this response, the processing plant owner decided to raise his processing fee 100% as a final offer. In other words, the agreement that was previously negotiated and the processing fee were no longer valid.

The new negotiator went back to the manager and advised him that the processing fee had gone up considerably. At this point, the manager had no choice but to ask my friendly talented negotiator to try to resurrect the previous terms agreed by the parties, which she did. At this point, it seems her negotiations skills with third parties were much better than her internal negotiating skills, which I pointed out to her post-mortem.

As you might have guessed, this negotiation destroyed the relationship between my good friend and her manager. They both shortly thereafter moved on to different positions (outside of negotiations). Losing her in the negotiations of further transactions in that company has cost the company significantly. (The company will never know... but I do.)

Another lesson here is, be careful about opening previously agreed-to terms and conditions. I have other examples of this lesson later in the book. I even have an example where the parties had to reopen previously agreed to terms to close the contract, but you have to read on to find this example and why.

Questions

1. What are the names of the key roles in the core negotiating team?

2. Why would you only want a negotiating team member responsible for handling action items for a contract?

3. What are subject matter experts and why are they necessary?

4. Why is it important to have regular communications between the negotiator/team and the decision maker?

5. What are at least three types of approval processes to allow a negotiating team to negotiate a contract?

6. What is the role of the Lead Negotiator in a negotiation?

7. What is the role of the Second Chair in a negotiation?

8. What is the role of the Analyst in a negotiation?

9. What is the role of the lawyer in a negotiation?

10. Who are the decision makers in your family and is the role split depending on what the issue is?

5
Gather Information

You have put together a team and have completed your initial framing, including issue raising. As part of issue raising, there are always a number of issues that need to be addressed.

Depending on where your project or contract will be performed, you have a number of important general issues to consider. We will take these one at the time.

Political Risk

You have decided to do business in a new country or country where some part of your company has done business. You need to understand the political risk. Understanding the rules and regulations of the industry that you are in is of great importance. However, some countries do not even have a regulatory structure in place. Depending on your relationship with the government, you may be able to help the government write the rules and regulations. Unfortunately, this can take a lot of time and expense educating government officials and decision makers. You may have to bear the expense for a third-party business expert that actually helps the government write its rules and regulations.

If you are negotiating a concession agreement with the government, you must put the issue of expropriation on the table (expropriation is a taking by the government of all or part of your assets or project). The government will maintain that you have no risk when it comes to expropriation. However, history is replete with examples where governments have expropriated assets from companies and individuals without fairly compensating them. There are a number of recent examples including Russia, Venezuela, and Argentina. Other forms of taking by governments include new taxes and regulations. You need to plan for these issues and have mitigation plans in place (if these are material issues).

Legal System

DISCLAIMER: I recommend you seek competent legal counsel. This section is only meant to inform you of some legal concerns.

In addition to political risk, there are legal risks from the government itself. Back in the 1970s, in the Middle East, contracts were not enforceable in some countries. The government may continue to negotiate terms and conditions after a company signs a contract. There may be no sanctity of contracts with these governmental entities.

In certain cases, the cost and enforceability of liens and arbitration could be prohibitive if the government wants all litigation and arbitration to be handled in country. Third parties (such as the World Court) are avenues for companies to enforce contracts if jurisdiction is agreed in advance of finalizing the contracts with these governments.

As stated above, some countries do not have regulations on whatever type of business you are trying to do in country. Therefore, you may want to choose law for your contract from a country that has very mature laws in the particular area, regardless of where you are doing business.

When it comes to maritime law, which country or state has the most developed law in this area? I always asked this question in my negotiation training course. Most people say New York but the correct answer is the United Kingdom. The British have been sailing ships for many centuries and have developed a very detailed and useful legal system when it comes to maritime law.

Another area of concern in dealing with other governments is waivers of sovereign immunity. Most governments have immunity from being sued. Thus, if you have a contract with a government or government owned entity that does not waive sovereign immunity, it will be difficult to enforce the contract. In business transactions, there may be a law or decree that allows for private entities to sue the government on certain business transactions. However, I would not rely on this, as laws can be changed and decrees can be revoked with a change in governments. Include a waiver of sovereign immunity and include an arbitration clause in another jurisdiction for your contract.

You might have had some exposure to the United States Foreign Corrupt Practices Act (FCPA). There are similar statutes in many other countries and these laws should not be taken lightly. I strongly recommend you review and make sure you understand what you can and cannot do in these countries. It is not my intent to explain the laws of other countries in this book, just to make you aware that you need to make sure that you know the laws and customs of other countries for your negotiations.

My Hummer

For instance, in certain countries "facilitating payments" are expected as part of any agreement that you are negotiating. Many years ago, one of my associates explained to me that the government agents he was negotiating with came in with the mistaken expectation that each would get a Hummer vehicle if the deal would go through. They were arguing over the color and he was at a loss what to do since he would have been fired if he lost the deal. What would you do in this situation?

I always recommend hiring a good lawyer before something like this happens to keep you out of jail...

Economics

You need to understand the value of your and your counterparty's key business drivers and issues. In one of my careers, I prepared economics for project negotiations. I also put together assumptions and economics for the counterparty to let the negotiating team know the value of an issue or item to the counterparty.

Your analyst should be putting together all the assumptions that go into your economics. These assumptions come from your subject matter experts on any of the issues that need to be addressed. Generate cash flow statements and generate earnings statements to better understand impacts. It is very important to have good tax counsel, not to just understand the taxes, but also to better understand the corporate tax structure.

Counterparty

If you do not have a credit group in your company, you may need to engage a third-party credit group to understand better the counterparty's credit and payment history. They should be able to gather data from various records even if you have to pay to get this information. Also, it may let you know whether you are going to have to finance your counterparty's or potential co-owner's transactions.

Regulatory Environment

You will need to determine what type of regulatory oversight that you can be subject to in country and if it is evolving and changing. If you are selling a product of some kind, you need to understand the rules and regulations that you will need to follow and the cost of doing business. This may include some type of licensing or permitting system.

In recent years, we have tried to license projects in California in the power industry. This has been extremely difficult, even though the state desperately needed the power. The same is true for Nigeria for different reasons. The former is due to regulatory constraints and the latter is because it can difficult to do business in Nigeria.

Tax, Foreign Exchange, and Currency

Now that you have decided to do business in a country, can you convert the local currency into whatever currency you need for your company? How easily will you be able to make distributions from your company, even if you can convert the local currency to your currency of choice?

The issue here is that you can come up with the best deal in the world, have great regulations and limited taxes, but get paid in local currency; however, you may not be able to convert the funds to another currency. As you might suspect, failure to handle the issue of currency controls can be very career limiting.

You find you can convert the currency into some other currency but now you are faced with another dilemma. You need to move the money out of the country. What do you do?

I have seen different forms of repatriation of funds, including by dividend or loans. Having good tax counsel should allow you to get the funds out of the country efficiently and legally for your company.

In all foreign transactions, your tax counsel should advise you on the tax structure that is most friendly to your transaction and your company under its home tax laws.

Understanding local taxes requirements can be difficult due to the number of taxes and requirements to buy locally. Locally available goods may be low quality and expensive in developing countries. Plan for these costs if you agree to have locally manufactured goods or use local labor.

In some countries, the tax fiscal terms may also be negotiable, depending on the industry. This is becoming rare, however, as the world moves towards more transparent markets.

Having good tax counsel is imperative in foreign transactions, regardless of where your company's home country is located.

Local Partner

A local partner or co-owner is necessary when you want to share some of the risks with a locally "connected" company or individual. Laws may require a local partner in some countries. Any local partner or co-owner needs to be financially capable and should have similar investment objectives as your company.

I know of transactions where we were looking to create a joint venture but our local partner had a very different set of decision and risk metrics. However, our executives still attempted to set up a joint venture.

It is the Economics, Stupid

On one occasion, the economics did not work for either party. However, the partner wanted to do the deal and try to fix the economics later. Fortunately, our management did not pursue that deal. We found out later the deal was only going to get worse, not better.

One of my favorite sayings is "Some of my best deals are the ones I did not do and destroy value." Unfortunately, we did some deals that did destroy value, and in some cases, lots of value.

My reputation throughout my career was that of a "fixer." I was sent in to fix problems or at least determine what the problems were in problematic projects or departments. As a negotiations teacher, some people ask for advice on how to fix negotiation problems created by others. Problems created by executives can be especially difficult.

Joint Ventures

Joint ventures are just like they sound, a business opportunity jointly taken with others who hopefully have the same agenda. Risks can be shared or limited by incorporating the business. There are many different types of corporate structures and again, your tax counsel should help you better understand the set-up of your business.

I have addressed some of the joint venture pitfalls in the prior sections. However, it is important to research whom you are doing business with and their underlying interests before you jump into a business arrangement. Joint ventures are a bit like marriage: much easier to get into than get out of when the deal is bad.

In addition to whatever contract you are negotiating for an existing project or joint venture, you must familiarize yourself with any issues in the main joint venture agreement.

If you are negotiating a joint venture or development contract, you will need to be concerned with a number of issues including management of the venture, ownership interest, dividend policy, deadlock and approval provisions, capital requirements, and potential for dissolution.

It is important to reconcile agendas and decision metrics early in a joint venture. Jointly framing the project may mitigate this since you should see where you are aligned and not aligned. Framing the project going forward is a little late to catch major misalignments but it will help to reconcile agendas and decision metrics.

Project Finance

If you have decided to finance your project, this means there are a lot of other people that want to know all about your project. Your approach to a negotiation will depend on a number of different factors, depending on whether the project is financed with debt or equity, or recourse or non-recourse financing. Banks will review the data in the economic model, specifically cash flow. In these instances, in addition to building an economic model, you will need to build a balance sheet, an income statement, and banking metrics for the banks review and information.

Since lenders generally do not take a lot of risk, your project will have to determine how much equity is required by the banks. This is mainly for non-recourse debt, meaning that the banks and lenders are limited to the project assets and do not have recourse to the assets of the owners of the joint venture project.

Internal and External Networks

If you are looking for something, "Google it" to see if you can find information on that particular subject or person on the Internet. It is interesting to find the amount of information on individuals, especially those with large egos or who are overly communicative.

Now with the proliferation of the Internet, there may be sources of information internal to your company and external through various websites. LinkedIn.com has a lot of information on business people that may be involved in your negotiations. If you are negotiating with particular project or company, there may be a significant amount of data on that project or company already on the Internet.

The Internet is a Wonderful Thing

I was negotiating with a counterparty's lawyer in a litigation case. I wanted to understand what assets the counterparty had. I was able to pay a relatively small fee through the Internet to obtain substantial information about the assets that my counterparty owned. I even ran across a recent tax foreclosure on one of the properties previously owned by the counterparty. The funds were available to the counterparty from this particular county due to the foreclosure. When I advised the lawyer, it appeared that the lawyer and, possibly, their client did not know about the tax foreclosure. This piece of information let me know the business acumen of my counterparty and its lawyers, or lack thereof.

Something else I have done in the past is to set up internal company networks that allowed negotiating teams to ask questions of other subject matter experts around the world. There were certain communication rules in place to inhibit confidential information from being shared. However, anyone could ask a question of the other 350 members of the employee network. The answers from the subject matter experts were handled directly with the party asking the question instead of over the network itself due to confidentiality concerns.

Gathering information is an essential part of any negotiation: the more you know, the more power you have. Go forth and become powerful!

Questions

1. What is expropriation and what are the different types?

2. Why would you need to understand the legal system of the country in which you are planning to operate?

3. What are some of the legal risks of doing business in any country?

4. What type of laws would you look at to determine the corporate structure for a new project or activity and why?

5. What are some ways to make distributions from companies to shareholders or stakeholders?

6. Why would you need a local partner?

7. What are some of the key issues that should be addressed in a partnership or joint venture?

8. What is non-recourse debt?

9. Why would you want to develop a network of contacts?

10. What sources of information would you use to find out information on a counterparty or anyone for that matter?

6
Negotiation Positions and Strategies

At this point in the negotiation process, you have setup your team, you have prepared a frame of the negotiation, you started gathering some of the information you need, and you are ready to start creating a contract.

Before you start populating a contract, develop a position table. Your opening positions are really a function of your most important objectives and bottom lines on each issue, along with your concession strategy. A position table will allow the negotiating team to discuss in detail each issue prior to determining an opening position.

Table 6.1, a Position Table, helps you set up the key issues you should address prior to populating any commercial contract. A more complete version of this document is in the Appendix and also addresses alternatives to the contract you will negotiate.

Let us briefly go over the top part of the position table regarding underlying interest and power.

Underlying interests are those business drivers for each party to complete the transaction you are negotiating. Underlying interests drive the decisions of all parties on the positions they take in the contract. For instance, the Japanese may be buying liquid natural gas to generate electricity, but their underlying interest is to provide electricity to the country.

Power comes in many forms, but simply it is the ability to influence others. You are mainly concerned here with who and what can impact your negotiations materially.

Position Table			
You: Underlying Interests (drivers) Power / Ability to Influence		Your Counterparty: Underlying Interests (drivers) Power / Ability to Influence	
Issue	You: 1. Desired outcome 2. Bottom line 3. Opening position	Counterparty: 1. Desired outcome 2. Bottom line 3. Opening position	Notes

Table 6.1: Position Table Template

We will cover underlying interests and power in more detail later. Both underlying interests and power are overarching issues for all the issues in the agreement.

Once you have considered underlying interest and power, you are ready to start preparation of negotiation positions in the position table.

You should have a good list of key contract issues in the framing document at this point. I suggest you use those issues as a starting point for your position table. Some of these issues may not rise to the level of what you are looking for in the initial negotiation document. You will need to decide the form of document that you are negotiating:

♦ Term Sheet,
♦ Memorandum of Understanding,
♦ Heads of Agreement (HOA), or
♦ A Comprehensive Binding Agreement.

For example, an asset divestiture negotiating team should consider focusing on putting together a preliminary contract instead of using a term sheet to start the negotiations. This will give your team leverage as a starting point with all the bidders.

Agreeing on the form of the agreement to be negotiated by the negotiating team must be completed prior to meeting with the counterparty. Therefore, I included a detailed discussion of many of the various types of contracts in Chapter 1.

Now that you have populated the position table with the issues from the framing document, discuss any new contract issues that you have discovered since you prepared the negotiation frame. Once you have completed this exercise and have sorted issues based on preliminary order of importance, look at each individual issue and determine the following:

1. Your most desired outcome on the issue. This is the best outcome you could expect on this issue. It does not have to be completely reasonable. However, you must be able to argue for this with a straight face or, in other words, you will not be laughing at your own reasons while you are explaining your position.

2. Your bottom line on the issue. It is the amount or value on this issue that you would go no lower as a seller or no higher as a buyer. Stated another way, if the counterparty wanted more on this particular issue than you are offering, you would rather walk away rather than continue with the negotiations. This is typically limited to key issues in your contract (or something that is not technically feasible).

   However, many times negotiators may say it is their bottom line, but in actuality, they may be bluffing. This is a different issue altogether. We will get into this in the later sections of the book when we discuss rules and tactics.

3. Your opening position on an issue. Opening positions are just like they sound. These are the terms and conditions you want to start discussing to try to get to your most desired outcome on each issue. An opening contract may be a term sheet or an initial complete contract addressing most of the issues.

Negotiators and lawyers many times populate contracts with their opening positions without clearly understanding the most desired outcome, bottom lines, and concession strategy on each issue. They may have negotiated these terms and conditions many times, believing they are prepared. However, thorough preparation will help you to do better.

Negotiating Strategies

Negotiating strictly using a contract may lead to negotiating each issue sequentially. This is not always ideal. I have negotiated using a position table or other tools to avoid a particular issue due to its potentially explosive nature. You can jump around in a contract to handle different issues since you should script the contract real time. Remaining flexible is a necessity.

Be sure to get alignment of your negotiating team on all the key issues by using the position table. This should lead to better discussions and outcomes. You will still negotiate with your counterparty most of the time using a contract.

The position table will allow you to document how you want to make concessions on a particular issue. You may want to negotiate other issues in the agreement at the same time since they are related or have similar values.

After you have prepared your side in a position table, you need to try to understand your counterparty's wants and needs. The better you understand the counterparty's needs and wants before each meeting with your counterparty, the more prepared you are to counter its arguments. Many people tend to focus solely on their own needs and wants. However, it is important to plan for your counterparty's most desired outcome and opening positions.

Don't Get Mad, Get Even

A lawyer I worked with in Colorado told me that early in his career, he would get outrageous offers from his counterparty in litigation. He would get so angry he would blow up. He ultimately learned that it is better to counter their arguments with equally aggressive counteroffers since that was the dance in litigation. Many lawsuits settle right before trial due to uncertainties of trial. It should be noted that getting an early aggressive settlement offer is standard practice in the insurance industry in the United States. Do not be surprised when you get an aggressive offer when dealing with an insurance company.

You now need to understand what the value of each issue is to all parties. Some issues have value that is not calculated but may be very important. Other issues have calculated values. You should make note of important issues for yourself, but also make note of perceived value to the other party. You can also color code the position table for dependent issues or issues that you want to negotiate simultaneously (since they have similar values).

After you have populated the position table, it is time to populate the agreement that you will negotiate. Important: review both the agreement and the position table as a team after you meet with your counterparty. Keep both documents up to date to keep the team aligned on issues.

This is a bit more work than using just a contract to negotiate. However, you may leave substantial value on the table without the team discussions and coming to agreement internally. In the courses I teach, we prove that lack of doing your homework comes up time and time again as a weakness and a significant cost. Some negotiators are too lazy to complete a position table or are overly confident in their contract positions. They focus solely on the agreement preparation and thus may not have a good understanding of the value they are giving up as part of the agreement. Most lawyers are trained on legal terms and conditions and less on valuation issues. Engage the negotiating team and SMEs to understand each issue, including valuations.

A number of my negotiation students have provided feedback in later years that doing their homework made a significant difference in their business dealings. They truly believed their outcomes were significantly better by doing their homework before the negotiations. They also used a few tactics and rules along the way that helped as well. We will address rules and tactics starting in the later chapters. While the tactics and rules may not come naturally to you, if you are prepared and have done your homework, you have a lot more power and a higher likelihood of getting a good contract.

Role Playing and Game Theory

As part of your preparation, play devil's advocate – have one of your team members take the side of the counterparty to argue their points. Role playing is a good way to better understand your and your counterparty's arguments. For some reason, some cultures do not like to role play negotiations. You will benefit from role playing, especially on key issues. You will be surprised at how much better you will be prepared.

Game theory can also provide very valuable insight into to your counterparty's interests and constraints. *Game Theory for Business*[7] by Paul Papayoanou explains both framing and analytics associated with a game theory approach. A role play exercise after completing a game theory analysis will provide excellent preparation for the actual negotiation.

One last thing before we move on to the next chapter: while the previous six chapters are not that exciting, they are important chapters. *Please do not plan to fail by failing to plan.* Please do your homeowork!

Questions

1. What are the key items found in a position table?

2. What are underlying interests?

3. How do you think you get power over others in a transaction?

4. Why would you want to come up with your most desired outcome, bottom line, and opening position in that order?

5. What is a most desired outcome?

6. What is a bottom line on an issue?

---

7   Papayoanou, Paul, *Game Theory for Business: A Primer in Strategic Gaming*, Probabilistic Publishing, 2010.

7. Why would you want to use a position table in a nego-
    tiation with your counterparty?

8. What is the difference between a want and a need in
    setting up your positions?

9. Why would you want to try to understand the potential
    bottom lines and opening positions of your counter-
    party?

7

Negotiate Externally (The Dance)

It seems most negotiating books start with negotiating rules, tactics, or cultural issues regarding engaging your counterparty. This chapter will focus on meeting your counterparty.

In my experience, negotiators are generally overly anxious to meet with the counterparty without doing adequate homework. Negotiators want to meet with their counterparty to learn information instead of doing the homework. They may be under tight deadlines or their pay may be greatly affected if they do not complete the negotiations timely. I have also found deadlines in performance agreements drive behaviors that short cut and may lead to bad outcomes if not adjusted. This is something I have noticed more often than not.

The first meeting should be focused on meeting the counterparty to do introductions, sharing scripted or plan information, and getting information from your counterparty.

Negotiation of various terms and conditions in your agreement should wait until you have completed adequate homework. Both parties should be prepared to discuss those particular issues in detail. You also may need several information gathering meetings before either party is prepared to start discussing terms and conditions.

All meetings regardless of the potential agenda should be planned and organized. You have a meeting with your counterparty; what should you do?

Contact your Counterparty

Contact your counterparty and agree on a time and place to meet, the issues to be addressed during the meeting, and any needed parties from both sides. Also determine if your counterparty plans to have new or different people in the meeting so that you can prepare. There is no guarantee that they will not change their mind about who will attend from their side and not tell you. You have to decide if a change like this is intentional or not and what to do (if anything). Everything you do sets precedent for the next time and all subsequent interactions. Be wary of new unplanned changes, but you will need to adapt to changes and surprises as they almost always happen.

The preference is to meet at your own offices, but sometimes this is not possible or workable.

Time for a Change

In one instance, we were meeting in our offices and had been meeting in our offices without making substantial progress on the contract. Another problem we had on this particular contract was that English was not the main language spoken by a substantial majority of people attending the negotiation. In this example, because there had been no real progress for two years, I decided to change the dynamics of the negotiation. We started to meet at their lawyer's offices. We started drafting the contract in the local language. We hired a technical writer to convert the agreement to English. My lawyers interpreted the language for me in real time. On key commercial terms, I continued to negotiate in English. My lawyers handled most of the discussions in the local language for legal issues that I did not handle. We scripted in the local language since that was the controlling language legally.

After these changes, we started to make progress on the commercial, legal, and technical issues. I correctly assumed that the counterparty's subject matter experts were not that fluent in English. They were more comfortable writing in the local language. The counterparty was much more comfortable in their own lawyer's offices. This completely changed the dynamics between the parties. Overall, I was comfortable with the changes (except that the lawyer's building elevators were a bit claustrophobic and failed to work half the time).

When your negotiation is continuing to stall, try to figure out what is necessary to progress the agreement within reason. Do not hesitate to be creative.

Pre-meeting

Before meeting with your counterparty, have a pre-meeting with your negotiating team, reemphasizing their roles and responsibilities. You should discuss each of the issues that you plan to address during the negotiations that day. Decide who will lead the discussion of each issue. As discussed in the previous chapter, role playing and game theory can help you prepare during the pre-meeting.

Initial Meeting

You have shown up at your counterparty's office or their lawyers office for negotiations for the day.

Several of the counterparty business team members are sitting in a conference room as you come in. You introduce yourself and your team if you have not met before. Their lawyers are nowhere to be found. You find out it will be at least an hour or more before their lawyers are available. What do you do?

You are not really in negotiations yet. *Wrong!* You are *always* in negotiations.

You also have not planned to be in negotiations without their lawyers present and your lawyer present. Therefore, you should get to know your counterparty's business people. Try to find out what their likes and dislikes are, where they are from, and any local items of interest. Sports are usually good to discuss in just about any setting. Therefore, you should do some homework prior to arriving to see what is happening locally. Check the Internet on the counterparty for any information. Research LinkedIn.com to see what you can learn about the meeting's participants. Also, understand any cultural constraints prior to asking. Every culture is different; plan for it.

Their lawyers finally show up and you start negotiations. However, a new issue shows up that has not been discussed previously and you are not prepared to discuss. What do you do?

Negotiations are a like a chess game: when they make a move, you have to decide what your move will be. You may need to defer (table) an issue until you have had time to study it, especially if the issue is material or greatly offends you.

In one negotiation I completed, a new material issue came up every time we met with one counterparty. This had been allowed by the prior Lead Negotiator. I did stop this from happening, but it took some time to change their behavior.

However, you will need to decide the best course of action. You can step out of the room for a while to prepare with your team to discuss the issue if it is important. If the issue is material or could impact other issues to be negotiated, reserve the right to revisit the issue at a later date. Many times, it is best to defer (table) discussion of any new unplanned issue until your team is prepared.

You have tabled the new issue and you have moved on to the issues that you want to address for that day. Some issues you need to address at some point include: their deadlines, approval process, potential decision-makers, and decision metrics. This will help you get both the best deal you can but also will allow you to better understand your counterparty's needs. Getting this information generally will not be easy. Depending on whom you are dealing with, your counterparty may be ready, willing, and able to give you all this data and more. Ask questions and *avoid interrupting your counterparty*. Take notes if you want to say something and then bring it up later. Allow your counterparty to give you information. Information is power, even if it is not what you want to hear.

After the Initial Meeting

You finish the day of negotiations with your counterparty. You have done your duty by persuading the other side of your positions. You have listened to their arguments all day. It is highly recommended that you draft the agreement real time with your counterparty. It will make it harder for them to say later that they misunderstood the discussion, especially if they helped prepare the comments.

When do you table a draft agreement? Set an agenda with your counterparty before the first meeting with the counterparty of the items you both agree to discuss. After the first meeting or when agreed, table a draft outline of the contract terms or general heading of issues to be finalized in a contract.

While it is recommended you control the drafting of the contract, the counterparty may want to control the drafting. In these situations, suggest to the counterparty that you let the lawyers sort out who will handle the drafting. The lawyers will agree on how the drafting will be handled. Generally, the lawyer with the most commercial experience will do the drafting. Having one party control the drafting of the agreement will help with versions. If you control the drafting, it will make sure you are aware of all changes since the last version.

Regardless of who controls drafting, your counterparty will send you a version with tracked changes at some point. Compare the current version to the prior version to see if there are changes from the prior version that were not noted or tracked. Your counterparty might make changes to an agreement without letting you know; compare every time.

What can go Wrong?

Sometimes in your negotiation meetings, things go horribly wrong for any number of reasons. For instance, the other party is continuing to be irrational, at least in your opinion, or the counterparty has an excellent counter argument to an issue you need. What do you do?

The best answer here is generally get out of the room or somehow table the issue for a later discussion. I know several negotiators that have some type of signal to their team to call a break instead of the lead negotiator. You do not want to appear weak at this point. However, you may want to just call a break to leave the issue open with your counterparty.

The World is Your Stage

I remember one time when we were in the middle of negotiations of a contract. I flew in the cramped economy section of a small plane for half a day to the location. The Lead Negotiator did not show up for the negotiations, but his negotiating team did. I later learned he was not planning to show up during the entire two-week period we were supposed to be negotiating the transaction.

I walked into the room. I noted that the counterparty's Lead Negotiator was not there. My local lawyers had not advised me. This was a strange negotiation anyway, as I was not the key contact on these agreements. My local counsel set up the meetings and coordinated the discussions.

The first thing I asked when I sat down was, "Where is your Lead Negotiator?" Of course, they responded that "He would not be at these meetings. We could tell them anything and everything we wanted and why." They would then discuss our position with their Lead Negotiator later. However, they were not there to negotiate anything, but willing to listen to us.

At this point, I looked at my local counsel. I said think we need to step out for a caucus. We stepped into the next room and then a nice loud voice I asked, "WHAT THE HELL AM I DOING HERE? I FLEW ALL THIS WAY FROM HOUSTON AND THEY ARE NOT GOING TO NEGOTIATE. WHAT A WASTE OF TIME." My lawyers were trying to calm me down. I actually was not really that upset, but I wanted to make sure that the counterparty knew of my displeasure. We had already been negotiating for months.

We then went back into the room and the counterparty's tune changed quite a bit. They were much more open to discussing the issues. They did say they could not agree to any of the issues without their Lead Negotiator signing off on the issues. However, they said that they had a good handle on the issues. They did not believe that there would be any pushback from their Lead Negotiator.

My reaction to their original message changed their demeanor to allow us to accomplish and close some of the issues that would have remained outstanding for several more months. We had been negotiating for a number of months at this point. I believe we had developed a fairly good rapport with all of their negotiating team. I am not sure this would have worked had we not be negotiating with the counterparty for some time.

Team Debrief

So you finished your meeting with your counterparty. You head back to your office or hotel. At this point, you are likely somewhat exhausted after several hours (and perhaps many days) of negotiating. You still need to debrief your team on what happened. Did anyone hear or see anything different than what was discussed? Update the position table, including documenting discussions on the issues.

Debriefing right after the meeting will allow you to be better prepared for the next pre-meeting with your negotiating team. You can update your position table, inform management of your progress, and document action items. Make sure that issues and new information are properly researched with subject matter experts or others as needed.

The Next Day

The next day comes and you start all over again. Hopefully, you are discussing additional or new issues and not the same ones every day. However, you may discuss the same issue for many days in a row, depending on how critical the issue is to the parties.

Negotiations are a lot of hard work but also can be fun for those that enjoy the challenge. I cannot stress enough how important it is to do your homework and being prepared for every interaction with your counterparty. It will certainly seem much less fun when you have bad outcomes due to poor planning. Also, not coming to agreement may be the best outcome if your agreement will destroy value. Good luck with your negotiation adventures!

Questions

1. Why would you want meetings to get information only?

2. You are having a meeting with your counterparty. What should you do to plan and prepare for the meeting?

3. Why do you think there a preference when negotiating with a counterparty to meet at your own office?

4. Why would you have a separate meeting with your negotiating team directly after meeting all day with your counterparty?

5. Why would you have a meeting with your negotiating team before each meeting with your counterparty?

6. What should you do when a new important issue is brought up in a meeting with your counterparty that you are not prepared to discuss?

7. What are some key general issues that need to be addressed with your counterparty? (This applies to any business negotiation.)

8. What do you think a typical "day" of negotiation looks like for a well-prepared negotiating team?

9. What is the most important part of a negotiation to get to a better outcome and close?

10. Why would you want a meeting agenda and objectives?

8
Close and Plan the Transition

Depending on the nature of the contract, the closing can be a big deal. Whoever is executing the agreements may need a Power of Attorney in order to execute the contracts properly. This is because the signer may not have the delegation of authority in their corporation. Usually, the lawyers on all sides are at the closing to review the documents to make sure that the terms and conditions match what had been negotiated previously.

Trust by Verifying

I remember one instance when I received a draft contract back from the counterparty during the negotiations that had been changed, but the changes had not been marked or tracked and my lawyer failed to catch the changes. I did the comparison of the prior contract to the current contract. I was just a bit upset that the counterparty would change something that we discussed without telling us. More importantly, I was upset that my lawyer did not catch it. In MS Word® (and probably other software), you can compare electronically the versions of the contract to look for changes that were not noted in the tracked or highlighted changed agreement.

On receiving every agreement, I always do a comparison with the prior document to see if there are any changes by the counterparty that have not been noted. Completing a clean version of the contract without tracked changes makes it easier to read and should be provided. A second version of the contract should be provided that highlights changes from the prior version in a separate document.

There have been a number of instances where we negotiate what we thought were clear terms and conditions. The counterparty, if an operator, may interpret the terms and conditions differently or may not appear to be applying the terms appropriately. Hopefully you put in strong language your right to get data if you think the operator is not complying with the contract terms.

The Data Shortage

We had one joint venture where the operator had interpreted the contract differently than the wording intended in the agreement. I asked one of my commercial negotiators to help the country manager since she was involved in negotiating the agreement for the operator. She must have done a good job for the operator since the terms of that contract made it difficult for us to get data on operations of the project. The terms and conditions may have been ambiguous enough for alternative interpretations as well. You can write a great contract but if you do not provide access to the information to check, it may not matter.

If your counterparty is the operator under your contract, they almost always interpret the contract much more favorably to them than to you. Therefore, it is extremely important that you understand every aspect of the contract. It is just as important to have the ability to prove non-compliance as it is to have clear wording in your contract.

Transition

Transition planning can be complicated, depending on the nature of the contract. Since most contracts are transitioned to operations, include examples of how the formulas work as attachments to the contract for operations to better understand. Sometimes the wording can be a bit confusing to people who were not involved in the negotiation.

If it is a business being transitioned, other services may be required to transition the assets to the new owner. Separate teams may be negotiating aspects of the transaction simultaneously in ancillary agreements to the overall sale of assets or stock. These are usually for fairly large transactions and extra resources may be needed.

For smaller transactions, much of this can be planned in detail with the key transition managers after the final main sales contract is completed. Transition managers may be members of the negotiating team, SMEs or new to the transaction once the main negotiations are completed. Anti-trust issues may prevent transition of intellectual property until final approvals are received from the appropriate government.

Legal counsel should always be involved in some form for major transactions, including the transition planning.

Questions

1. Why would you review and compare a contract received from your counterparty against a prior draft of the contract?

2. Why would you need a power of attorney to sign a contract?

3. At closing, who should review the contracts and why?

4. What is transition planning for a contract and why would you do it?

5. Why would a government need to approve an asset sale?

6. When would a counterparty interpret contract terms more favorable to them than what was intended?

9
Negotiation Planning Rules

While we did address the planning of negotiations in prior chapters when discussing the overall negotiation process, it is equally important to understand the rules of negotiation for each phase of negotiations along with the tactics and truisms of negotiations. In this chapter, we will address planning rules. The examples will help you to better understand the rules.

1. Always Do Your Homework!

Set up your overall commercial team, including the negotiating team and non-core team members. Non-core members are generally subject matter experts.

Develop a frame that includes agreeing on the opportunity, what success looks like, boundary conditions, objectives, decisions, issues, facts, decision metrics, uncertainties, risks, and action items. A frame is an organizational tool that allows you to better understand and agree on your approach to the negotiations.

Seek information to populate the position table with your most desired outcome, bottom line, and opening position on each key issue. A detailed position table can be found in the Appendix. Using this tool will allow you to better understand each issue as a team. The drivers or underlying interest and power considerations for you and your counterparty should also be documented in the position table. At the bottom of the position table, include any alternatives to the negotiation, if they exist.

There is a lot of publicly available information on the Internet. There are numerous sources to look at for information, including government websites, counterparty company websites, social media sites, and general searches of the Internet for information. Additionally, your internal team members will have valuable information regarding your negotiations that should come out in the framing session and meetings. With smaller public companies, you may be able to search the US Securities and Exchange Commission's website for material.

Develop your and your counterparty's negotiation positions and strategies using a position table. Start documenting in the position table what you think you and your counterparty will want on key issues, including most desired outcomes, bottom lines, and even expected opening positions. You will also need to document underlying interests, power considerations, and potential alternatives to agreement.

People do not think about their counterparty's needs or wants until much later or too late. This is a mistake. Negotiating teams are generally focused on what they want and need. You need to understand what your counterparty wants and why they want it in order to get to an agreement in some form.

That is a Bunch of Scrap

One time we were negotiating the use of a large drilling rig in the 1980s. The drilling rig was sitting idle and had no apparent alternative uses for the indefinite future. When I ran economics for that drilling rig, I assumed that the rig had the value of scrap. We then proceeded to put together a set of economics for our counterparty that included a significant amount of cash flow for use of the drilling rig. Needless to say, the counterparty strongly disagreed with our valuation of the drilling rig, but they got the point. We were able to get a substantial discount on use of the drilling rig during the contract term.

Keep the position table updated so that your negotiating team stays aligned and include any new information. The position table also should document the current state of any outstanding issues and who is handling.

- ◆ Differentiate between small and big issues by understanding the values or importance to all parties.
- ◆ Understand your positions and the points that you are willing to "trade," including related issues for you and your counterparty.
- ◆ Stress what is needed for each issue (bottom line) versus what is wanted. This is especially an issue when dealing with subject matter experts and management.

2. There is a correlation between aspiration level and outcome: if you do not ask for it, chances are you will not get it.

Do not settle for bottom lines on key issues. There are studies that suggest people tend to settle at bottom lines much too often since it is safe. Managers also need to hold their negotiating teams accountable to achieve better results than bottom lines on key issues.

Conversely, setting too aggressive opening positions will make your negotiations much more difficult and create a higher probability of deadlock.

Negotiating teams should provide management with enough information to allow the manager to give some authority to the negotiating team to negotiate.

Companies and managers should set bottom lines for negotiating teams above their real bottom lines to achieve better outcomes. This also forces negotiating teams to come back to management if they have to go beyond the authorized bottom line to seek approval on a key issue.

3. Determine your authority to negotiate.

There are different ways to seek approvals in corporations. While these are discussed briefly earlier in the book, I would like to reiterate several different approaches. The right one for your negotiations may be different each time (depending on the type of negotiations).

- Complete the full negotiation with only final sign off by management. This is risky. Unless your manager has absolute confidence in you, this is generally a big mistake since your manager or executive may disagree with the outcome you attained.

- Seek full negotiation authority of management of key negotiation terms and conditions prior to negotiations, but come back to management if you need to exceed bottom lines. This is also called getting a *mandate*.

  This allows the negotiating team to negotiate as long as the team stays within the agreed-to management bottom lines. Getting a mandate to negotiate is the norm in the liquid natural gas (LNG) industry. Generally, when an LNG contract is negotiated, the current key terms and conditions are well known in the industry from recent contracts. These recent contracts act as an anchor for then-current LNG price negotiations.

- Have a key contact in management who has approval authority to review your negotiation as it progresses.

  This worked out well when we were selling assets and technologies. Since it was important to executive management to be involved in these larger transactions, it was best to have the executive in charge of that particular area of the company briefed on an ongoing basis as we sold the assets and technologies. However, we were very careful to keep the executive out of the room and out of the negotiations with our counterparty.

  Many executives may not be available to handle the demands of being involved with a team in negotiations. As an alternative to continuous interactions with executive management, go back to management for approval to go below a bottom line on any key issues at the same time. You may be able to resolve an issue later in your negotiations.

The Delayed Participant

We were negotiating with a large multi-national company on an agreement for one of our projects for many months. We had agreed to seven out of nine key issues in the agreement. Our lead negotiator recognized that neither party could move on the last two issues. When our lead negotiator told the counterparty that we needed to ask our managers to resolve the last two issues, the counterparty said, "If you do that, then all of the issues are open, not just the last two."

Our lead negotiator had run into a roadblock he could not pass. When he asked for my advice, I told him that the counterparty wants to delay our project for some reason. This was a very material contract to move the project forward. However, I also thought they might not want to exit the project, so delay was preferred.

We discussed the possibility that the counterparty did not have the expenditures in budget to move forward at this time since they were in process of building a very similar large project. Interestingly, he did finally get the counterparty to come to terms at a later date and the project proceeded.

♦ The riskiest approach is negotiating with full authority. Executives, individual business owners, and other individuals need to learn how to limit their authority.

Some suggestions to limit your authority include:

♦ Look to a partner or spouse for final approval,
♦ Use cost as a limiter (even if you have the funds), or
♦ Indicate that your bank would not approve (if you have a lender).

Many times, executive management negotiates deals or concessions and achieves closure with poor outcomes for their companies. Executives and senior managers generally do not have the time or do not make the time to prepare. As a double jeopardy issue, they also have too much authority. I have said throughout my career: *executives and subject matter experts may give away the ranch even if well prepared by the negotiating team.* They have too much power or too much information. Even so, prepare your executives and subject matter experts for any interaction with your counterparty, including making sure they understand their role and the desired outcomes.

It can be career limiting to stop your executives from wasting company resources. However, I have successfully stopped management on several occasions. It is all about the trust management and executives place in your judgment, which takes time to establish.

Negotiating with Hitler

A keen example of having too much authority was prior to World War II when the UK Prime Minister Chamberlain, in negotiations with Hitler, gave away substantial concessions and thus paved the way for millions of people to die during that war. Today, game theory would have helped Chamberlain better understand the trade-offs with each concession he was prepared to make (i.e., what Hitler might do next).

As noted earlier, there is a good book called *Game Theory for Business: A Primer in Strategic Gaming*[8] by Paul Papayoanou that I highly recommend. Game Theory can help you prepare for negotiation, as it can really help you understand your counterparty's position and constraints.

Always limit your authority to your bottom lines that you have developed, regardless of how you are negotiating the agreements. Those negotiators that do not develop their bottom lines can never go below their bottom lines since they do not exist. However, there is a high probability of destroying value when bottom lines are not developed and well understood.

---

8   Ibid.

4. Understand the authority of your counterparty.

Understand who has power in your counterparty's company:

- ♦ What is the counterparty's approval process to negotiate the deal?
- ♦ Do they have to go back to management on every issue or were they granted the power to negotiate?
- ♦ Determine if you have individuals in your company who can contact the other company for information.

Keep management informed. Their management may call your management to override your negotiation positions. This is a problem in just about every industry because every industry is in reality a fairly small community. You will run into the same people over and over again in your industry. I ran into a banker checking into a hotel at 3:00 AM in Singapore that I worked with in Brazil a number of years earlier in my career. He lived in London at the time. I lived in Houston.

I have said many times: *It is not what you know, it is who you know.* This is another one of my personal rules. I was not the originator of this saying, which is probably a thousand of years old.

What are your and your counterparty's approval authority processes?

- ♦ Who has delegation of authority to sign the contract and commit resources?
- ♦ Who else will need to approve the content in your contract? You may have a need for insurance, credit, or another internal department to approve the language you are including in your contract. Also, these internal departments may want additional contract language or point out additional required approvals. Do not wait until the contract is final to engage your internal departments.

Don't Panic, Negotiate

I was negotiating a product sales contract for a company. I called a consultant I knew in the credit group to discuss what they needed to approve the agreement. I advised him of the terms and conditions of the deal we were working at that point in the negotiations. There was still a lot of work to do, but the value (potential accounts receivable) was relatively set. It was not a material contract to the company. The agreement was with our joint venture co-owner on a major capital project, who was also the purchaser of the product in the contract we were negotiating. At the time, I was told there was no need to run a credit report, nor was there a need for the credit group to be involved. Stupidly, I went on my merry way.

After we negotiated the terms and conditions of the sales contract, my credit group came back to us with extremely onerous language. They told us this language had to be included in the contract, otherwise they would not approve the contract for execution.

I thought, "I am a negotiator; do not panic, negotiate." In large companies, your most difficult negotiations are generally internal negotiations with other departments, including insurance, accounting, treasury, tax, and legal.

I knew someone in high places in that group so I called him to see if he could assist. I explained the facts and circumstances surrounding the agreement. I explained how little value this agreement was compared to the overall structure of the deal that had been negotiated and the product to be sold. I also explained that we had completely negotiated the agreement and both parties had approved the agreements.

After a bit of haggling, I was able to keep the clause out of the contract and close on the terms we had agreed.

5. Cap liabilities and avoid tax indemnities (when possible).

Executives and investors are happy when the market is good in any industry and executives tend to plan for good times.

The opposite is true during bad times in most industries. For this reason, planning for both the upside and the downside in any contract is an important part of doing your homework.

I have seen material problems in the oil and gas industry every few years throughout my career when the market turns down. It is a bit frustrating telling people to plan for the downside when things are good. They do not listen.

In the oil and gas industry, companies have renewed leases for assets like drilling rigs without understanding the longer-term prices needed to be economically viable. Since everyone has their own company price deck, they cannot share prices due to anti-trust issues. If you blindly follow a price deck, you get what management wants with that price deck. In times of significant price volatility, price decks tend to lack meaning and investments should be run at various levels to see what the best investments are, if any.

The poet and novelist, George Santayana, has philosophized that those who fail to study history are doomed to repeat it over and over again. I had a running joke that we prepare lessons learned every year, *which tended to be the same lessons we learned the prior year*. With this reasoning, how can lessons learned that recur year after year be lessons we have learned? I suggested, facetiously, that instead of calling them lessons learned we should call them, "Lessons we failed to learn and mistakes we continue to make."

If you look back in the energy industry, in the 1950s and 1960s, the energy industry overbuilt the chemical business. In the 1970s and 1980s they overbuilt the refining industry. In the 1990s and the first half of the decade of 2000s, they overbuilt LNG regasification facilities. In the last part of the 2000s and the decade of 2010, they overbuilt LNG liquefaction. If nothing, the energy industry consists of consistently poor planners. This is likely to happen in other industries, including in electric and self-driving cars. I am sure the energy industry has not learned its lesson.

6. Focus on underlying interests of your counterparty, not just contract positions.

While we are very good at documenting each of the positions on different issues, we also need to focus on why the counter-party is taking various positions in the contract. This leads to better understanding of their underlying interests.

At the top of the position table, there is a section to document both your counterparty's and your underlying interests. Underlying interests are those needs and wants of the parties that override the entire contract positions of each party. If one party does not meet the underlying interests, then there is no deal to be had regardless of the amount of negotiations that takes place. Understanding your counterparty and the underlying interests of your company are essential to get to a better deal for both parties. You also may discover something that can move the contract along if you get deadlocked.

The way to try to find out your counterparty's underlying interest is to ask why they need something. You may need to ask several times. This is also called root cause analysis, which is also known as the "Five Whys." When you look at a contract, it states the current position or positions of the party. It generally does not state the underlying interests of the parties to the contracts.

Children are very good at asking why many times. Parents find asking why is very annoying since our children tend to do this over and over again to us. Also, "because I said so" is not a proper response when you are dealing with an adult; it does not work with children either. You will be surprised at what you might find out if you just ask "Why?"

The Why Guy

For example, I had a conversation with my son a number of years ago. It went something like this. I told him, "You need to do your homework." His response was of course, "Why?" My answer was, "You need to get good grades in high school."

His response was" Why?" I then told him, "You need good grades to get into a good college." His response was (and you guessed it), "Why?"

I told him, "In addition to getting good grades in high school, he needed to learn enough so he could get good grades in college." His response was again, "Why?"

I told him, "You need to get a degree and graduate from college. You need good grades in high school at a minimum to be able to get good grades in college." And again, he asked me "Why?" I then had to tell him my underlying interest or real reason for telling him to get good grades in high school. What do you think I told him?

I told him that I loved him dearly to start. However, I really wanted him to start generating his own money so he could support himself instead of me supporting him. (This sounded funnier when I told this story in my class.)

Table 9.1 shows a contract position and then lists a potential underlying interest of the counterparty. This should also give a better understanding of positions in an agreement versus what are the potential underlying interests of your counterparty. In the first example we see that the buyer will not pay more than a certain amount for product. There could be a number of reasons why the buyer would not pay more, e.g., the buyer has other alternatives that are equal to or better than what the seller is offering.

Examples of Positions versus Underlying Interests	
Contract Position	Potential Underlying Interest
Buyer will not pay more than a certain amount for a product.	Buyer has other alternatives.
Buyer is unwilling to get higher management involved to solve last key issue in major contract.	Buyer wants to stall implementation on major project.
Seller wants to close quickly.	Seller has deadline on its performance agreement.

Table 9.1: Contract Positions versus Underlying Interests

Many times, in contracts, we include *recitals* in the front of the contract. A *recital* is a formal statement appearing in a contract or other legal document that provides an explanation of the objective of the transaction. In sales contracts, we include the comment that the buyer is buying a certain product and the seller is selling that product to the buyer. However, there may be a number of other reasons the buyer or seller wants the transaction. This is a higher-level response of both parties of their underlying interests. However, be careful and consult your lawyer before you agree to a recital in your contracts. In some countries recitals become a binding part of the agreement and can force unforeseen damages or change the nature of the agreement.

7. Do not open with your bottom line on key issues.

The reasons you do not open at bottom lines on key issues include:

♦ In business, your counterparty is generally expecting a fairly aggressive opening position if they are used to negotiating. Therefore, their counteroffer will generally be significantly different than your opening positions. You generally will be unsuccessful at negotiating from your opening offer if it is your bottom line. It will stall your negotiations and may make the agreement a win-lose contract, which is unacceptable in many cultures.

♦ The counterparty will think you are difficult to deal with or do not understand what you are negotiating when you will not come off your opening position.

Opening at bottom lines is of great concern when dealing with people who are schedule driven like project managers, managers, or executives. They want you to complete your negotiations since they may have completing the contract on their performance agreement for the current year (it may also be in your performance agreement for the current year). Choose your words carefully in your performance agreements. You will be punished at the end of the year if do not meet your objectives. (However, you may be punished anyway, even if you word your performance agreement appropriately.)

In the project world, some projects have many contracts that need to be negotiated as part of the overall project. The project manager generally will be managing overall activities on a project with a project team. Your contract may be one of many contracts or many activities on a particular project that need to be completed. The project manager does not want your contract to be on the critical path of his or her project. Therefore, he or she may put an inordinate amount of pressure on you to close and potentially destroy value in the project.

Negotiators must not be perfectionists. We must close with an imperfect contract, especially if further negotiations will not materially add value. This is a balancing act. You need to understand any material downside to closing and finalizing the contract. Your manager many override any concerns to force you to finalize your agreement. That is life in the business world!

Unfortunately, later material contract problems that arise will be blamed on you as Lead Negotiator of the agreement. That is also life. It is better to be lucky in this circumstance to get to close because being smart may not help you close. Hopefully, you are both lucky and smart.

8. Understand your counterparty's culture.

I am not an expert on culture and never will be. The main book on culture I recommend is called *Kiss, Bow or Shake Hands.*[9] You can review the main book or the specific country book in the series prior to any engagements with third parties from different countries. I suspect Google's youtube.com is also a place you can find much of the same information. I am not sure how reliable this information is on the Internet (but that is a discussion for another time). The books on a specific culture have more information than you can get from just reading the highlights in their main book on cultures.

I also recommend reaching out to co-workers and friends with experience in the country. You can get insights on the people, your counterparty, and the culture.

---

9   Morrison, Terri, and Conaway, Wayne, *Kiss, Bow or Shake Hands*, Second Edition, Adams Media (2006).

The Cultured Presenter

The first time I ever gave a presentation on negotiations to a large audience (150 or more people), I felt the presentation went extremely well. After the presentation was over, my friends from South America told me that I missed the most important aspect of negotiations. Needless to say, this was devastating to me. I said, "I think I covered just about everything; what do you guys think that I missed?"

They understood that culture is one of the more critical aspects of any business negotiation. I omitted mentioning culture even once during my presentation. I will never forget my omission in the presentation. (It seems we remember our omissions or failures much more so that our successes, which is human nature.)

9. Discover and manage all deadlines.

Most projects have several sets of deadlines. These deadlines include what the teams advise externally through press releases, what the team discusses among the co-owners (each co-owner may have different deadlines), and the internal project team projected deadlines (i.e., when the project team thinks the activities will actually happen). If your contract is part of a larger project, then you may have another set of deadlines for your negotiating team.

Besides your team deadlines, other parties, like executives, may have on their agendas a need to close the contract.

There are Spies Everywhere

I ran into this issue when I was negotiating agreements in South America. We had been working on key terms and conditions on several contracts, three to be precise. And there was a penalty clause in one of the contracts that said, "... to be negotiated later." The agreement was supposed to be a memorandum of understanding, which is generally a nonbinding agreement. However, the counterparty in this case, the government, decided they wanted to fully negotiate this particular agreement. We had not touched that particular clause when they brought it up. I said, "We need to discuss it." I offered to eliminate that penalty provision from the contract since we were negotiating the penalty provisions in other areas. The counterparty came back with a very aggressive counteroffer.

The next morning, I received a call from our country manager, who started yelling at me about opening up that penalty clause in the contract. Fortunately, I did not work for the manager directly at the time. I was tempted to say (since he had not introduced himself), "Who is this?" However, I did not say anything. I continued to take the abuse for a little while longer over the phone.

I told him my reasoning for negotiating that particular clause in the contract, which did not impress him. I also told him at this point we needed to finish negotiating all the clauses in the contract. I also knew that my boss was probably going to get a phone call from someone at some point complaining.

We finished negotiating all of the "key" terms and conditions with the counterparty. The parties moved forward with the project prior to finalizing the contracts. However, the country manager made it clear to his people and ultimately to me that I was not necessary to negotiate the remaining terms of the contracts. I was to stay available for conference calls.

I do believe the country manager had also set deadlines with his employees and I missed the deadline, which was unknown to me. Let me be particularly blunt on the issue of deadlines. Deadlines are generally arbitrarily set and can be changed. Changes may cost money though. The parties may not tell you their actual deadlines, may tell you incorrect deadlines, or may not even have deadlines.

We did finalize those agreements on the South American project during the next several months. The project was successful. However, we did not meet the internal deadlines to complete the negotiations. There were also a lot of other minor issues that needed to be addressed prior to closing taking place on those particular agreements. Since this project did very well, the country manager was ultimately promoted and has done very well. However, in life, a poor project or bad contract is generally an orphan and is on you if you are the Lead Negotiator. The country manager and his predecessor incorrectly thought these contracts were immaterial, but I knew these contracts were critical to moving the project forward. Hence, it took more time to negotiate and blame was assessed, instead of credit, for finally finishing the agreements.

Not having deadlines is something we run into when dealing with governments. This is not true when dealing with government requests, however. Governments generally set very firm deadlines when they want something. I know many people, including myself, that have worked many hours to respond to government inquiries and requests. These are facts that do not change. However, there are ways to get the government to respond to your deadlines.

You Can Buy Time if You Know the Price

We were negotiating a business deal with a government over many months. It was very frustrating as the government mainly responded that they did not care for our offers. Additionally, we did work to determine that every month that we did not have an agreement, the government would lose one million dollars. This was apparently not compelling to the government department. We finally asked the government, "Why?" to determine their underlying interest. This would help us establish a deadline. We were concerned about quoting a price since there were a number of other government departments we needed to negotiate with to get a final price. The department we were dealing with at the time wanted the absolute lowest price quoted, even if other governmental fees and cost would be added to the final cost.

Hence, we found out their underlying interest. It helped us establish a deadline that did not exist previously. After working the issue for a short period of time, we closed, helping both our company and the government move forward.

Your job as Lead Negotiator is to find out and coordinate all deadlines with all parties as they relate to your particular contract. This may include your counterparty, the government, your project manager, your manager, your subject matter experts, and whoever else may need to approve the final contract.

Your job as Lead Negotiator is also to make sure that your project manager, manager, or executive are kept informed. You will need to understand the values and trade-offs of closing your contract early versus allowing negotiating beyond the deadline for your contract. Good luck; you will need it.

10. Always have a mitigation plan for potential risks.

A number of risks will come up during the framing of your negotiations and during negotiations with your counterparty.

You should maintain a risk register to keep track of risks to make sure they are addressed. A risk register should include a list of potential risks, the responsible person on your core team to address them, dates to be completed, and mitigation plans. Keep your risk register up to date so that you do not forget to handle these risks as part of your negotiations.

11. Find out as much as you can about your counterparty.

Search LinkedIn, Facebook, or other online sources. Identify who your counterparties are. United States (U.S.) registered companies must search the U.S. Department of Justice Easenet website to determine if an international party or company they are dealing with can contract with a U.S. company.

You should always try to determine whom you are meeting for every interaction with your counterparty.

There is a lot of information on the Internet. Google yourself to see what your counterparty can find out about you. Do not be surprised if they have information that you do not want them to have in today's open society.

Mitigate any information about yourself that can be found online. If you are part of an online social or work network, I suggest you limit what you say and how you say it. This information will be permanently stored and you may not even own the right to your information.

Having fun is part of negotiating and being prepared allows you to better enjoy negotiating!

Questions

1. What are the eleven negotiation planning rules?

2. What negotiation processes are included in doing your homework?

3. What are the key parts of a framing document?

4. Why would you want to populate a position table with your most desired outcome and bottom lines and your counterparty's potential most desired outcomes and bottom lines?

5. Why would you want to have aggressive opening positions?

6. What are some ways teams or negotiators can get power in negotiating terms and conditions in a contract?

7. Why would you need to understand your counterparty's negotiating authority or their approval processes?

8. Why should you consider capping liabilities or avoiding tax indemnities?

9. What are underlying interests?

10. What is meant by bottom line?

11. Why would you need to understand the culture of your counterparty?

12. What are the different types of deadlines a project may have?

13. Why would you want to maintain a risk register?

14. What are some ways to find out information about your counterparty?

10
Negotiation Interaction Rules

The negotiation interaction rules covered in this chapter are focused on what happens during the negotiations with your counterparty and in your internal negotiations within your company. You will be stressed at times and your emotions may make you question your planning. Following these rules will help you mitigate impacts of stress and emotions. These rules and examples may also help you understand why something happened in one of your past negotiations when you did not follow one or more of these rules.

1. There is only one Lead Negotiator on your side of the table.

Plan for other team members to talk about specific issues but agree in advance of the meetings who will negotiate which issues. The Lead Negotiator generally will defer to someone on the team to handle SME or legal issues, if necessary.

What happens if, in meeting with your counterparty, someone on your side of the table arrives unprepared or decides to discuss a new idea or solution not previously discussed as a team?

This can undermine your negotiations. Unprepared team members need to have a bit of your face time, one on one, to discuss a path forward. Ignoring problems generally does not get rid of them.

Thanksgiving Concessions

We were negotiating an issue and my lawyer inadvertently said that we could do this another way. He proceeded
to discuss a potential concession. I was willing to make this
concession but had not discussed it prior to our meeting. I
was more than a bit flustered, but it was partly my fault for
not telling my lawyer. I should have discussed the issue with
my lawyers prior to meeting with our counterparty. Also, I
give some blame to my lawyer. He should have called a caucus (i.e., a break) instead of offering a solution we had not
discussed. This would have allowed us to discuss solutions
to get the most value in return for the concession.

Since we spend a lot of time with our counterparties, we may
get too friendly in these negotiations and inadvertently let a
concession slip.

2. Have pre-meetings with your team, agree on the agenda with your counterparty, and debrief the team after each negotiation.

As I have discussed previously, you should:

♦ Have a pre-meeting with your negotiating team to
  get alignment on issues to be discussed that day prior
  to meeting with your counterparty.
♦ Agree on the next day agenda with your counterparty
  at the close of the day.
♦ Have a debrief meeting to see what the negotiating
  team heard and saw after you meet with your counterparty each day.

Your pre-meeting and debrief meetings should prepare you
for your next meeting with your counterparty. You should
get alignment on issues, role-play issues, and update action
items. Role-playing will help you to better understand counter
arguments on your positions.

During debrief meetings, learn what your team may have
observed and heard. Since the Lead Negotiator is talking most

of the time, the team may have picked up body language or heard something that the Lead Negotiator should know. If you are not scribing the contract in real time, prepare a short summary of what was agreed to at the meeting. Send your summary to your counterparty along with issues you hope to discuss at the next meeting if appropriate.

Keep your position table updated so that your negotiating team stays aligned on where you are going on the issues to be addressed that day. The problem with using only the contract to document your positions is that you may not remember where you wanted to go with a particular issue. Having a separate position table will help with sparking your memory.

Assume that your counterparty may be able to listen to your conversations if you are in their territory. Technology may also interfere with your ability to have offline conversations with others. Be aware of where you are and your surroundings, especially restaurants, hotels, and bars.

The Blind Bidder

We were traveling by plane to bid on a project for a government. In the seat in front of us, another group was working on the same project on their computer in plain sight of everyone on the plane including us. It was hard not to see what they were doing. While it did nothing to change our strategy and we did not consider any information we received, not everyone is that kind.

I remember another time we were bidding to purchase a government utility. Enron out-bid us by a very small margin. These were multimillion-dollar bids. I could only speculate that somehow, they had access to our data or they were very lucky.

No negotiation goes exactly as planned. If you do plan, you may get ahead of an issue and better understand the direction to take the negotiations.

3. Quid Pro Quo: seek information when giving information and a tradeoff for every concession.

Quid Pro Quo means getting a favor for a favor. The first issue regarding favors is sharing of information with your counterparty. How do we know what to share and when to share information? Information is power, so we are reluctant to share information. However, if you are selling something, you need to tell the buyer what you are selling. You also need to make a compelling case that the buyer needs to buy whatever you are selling.

If you are the buyer, you want the seller to understand what your needs are so the seller can meet them. However, you are always concerned that the seller will use this information against you.

The introduction process between the buyer and seller is the initial negotiation dance. In business development, it is generally understood that the seller's initial conversation on major transactions with a buyer should be fairly well scripted. The seller knows what they want to say and what information they want to share. Beyond that, it is the initial introduction of the parties. They are also trying to figure out whether they want to do business with each other. The buyer may not be as prepared since they may not have the details of what the seller is offering during the first meeting.

The other issue regarding doing favors is getting a concession for each concession you make (i.e., I give you a concession, I expect a concession from you). You may not always get a concession but you need to see what is available from the counterparty. Additionally, you will generally never get a concession unless you ask. A concession is not necessarily a compromise, especially when the issue is immaterial to both parties. I will discuss concessions and how to make them later in the book, but you need to be prepared to ask for something when you give up something.

Once you give up a concession without asking for something in return, that concession is old news. You generally cannot get anything for a prior concession.

Lastly, when the other party wants to win without conceding any issues, they probably have not prepared very well, they may have other well-defined alternatives, or they just may be difficult. Find out by asking why they need something or why they are unwilling to give you something. Regardless of their reasons, get ready for a difficult negotiation unless you can change the tone of the discussions.

4. Meet face to face; avoid email and telephone negotiations.

It is better to meet face to face and avoid negotiating by email, text messages or electronics. How many times have you sent an email and someone misunderstood what you were saying or took the email the wrong way?

Also, as the other party gets further away from you, literally by text or email, it is easier for them to say no or to ignore you.

Another reason to meet face to face is to attempt to read their body language. There is a book that I recommend, *Strictly Business: Body Language* by Jan Hargrave.[10] It makes so much sense to be sitting in front of your counterparty to look at their body language. You may be able to pick up clues by looking at how they are acting while negotiating. Of course, the opposite is true; your counterparty may be able to pick up clues from your body language.

Seek Help on Their Side

On one of many occasions, I was arguing with my counterparty's lead lawyer on a deal we were negotiating. I am not sure he understood the issue as English was not his native language, but he surely had "no" down and kept saying, "No." I started talking to the lead commercial business person at the same time (i.e., making eye contact). I explained in simple terms as best I could why we needed the clause or terms in the contract. Their lawyer kept shaking his head and saying "no" over and over again. The lead commercial person stated that, "Craig is right ..." on this particular issue. He then explained to their lawyers in their native language why I was right and we moved on.

I am not an expert on body language. If you read more on body language, you will be able to better understand some of

---

10 Hargrave, Jan, *Strictly Business: Body Language: Using Nonverbal Communication for Power and Success,* 2nd Edition, Kendall Hunt Publishing, 2009.

the nuances of what people are saying. Jan Hargrave told me that about 70 to 80% of communication is nonverbal. If you are paying attention only to the verbal communications, you are missing a significant part of the negotiations. Having phone or email-only conversations, you will miss the body language feedback of your counterparty and your counterparty will miss yours.

5. Question, question, question – both for clarification and information

As a manager or analyst, I was always in the questioning mode. The more you know, the more likely difficult situations or issues can be resolved with your counterparty. It might be a situation that cannot be resolved. The sooner you find out, the better, so that all can move on to other more productive activities.

Hearing What We Want to Hear

One of my colleagues told me about a meeting he had when both Lead Negotiators were agreeing on an issue. Neither Lead Negotiator listened to what the other party said. The Lead Negotiators were not asking questions of each other but were hearing what they wanted to hear. My colleague asked our Lead Negotiator to step out of the meeting and proceeded to tell him what the other party wanted. Our Lead Negotiator had no clue that what they wanted was very different from what he thought he was hearing. In this case, both parties spoke English as their main language. Just think about when an interpreter needs to used and the potential for confusion that occurs in translating to different languages.

I also gave an example earlier where we were asking for a particular property from the government. We were only told that they would not sell us that property but we could buy a piece of property further inland. We might have found connections in the government where we could find out additional information, but we had a fast approaching deadline. Our negotiators sought my advice on getting the government to sell us the property. I simply asked, "Why" they thought the government was holding out. They strongly believed that the government wanted to sell to a another buyer that paid more local taxes than our project would ever pay. I advised our negotiators to find another site since the government was never going to sell them the property they wanted. You generally cannot make someone sell you something unless you have some power granted by law.

Do not be afraid to ask for more information and to ask why. It is the question that is not asked that can get us into trouble.

6. If you cannot be truthful, it is best not to say it; be ethical.

You should never lie to your counterparty, but alternatively, you should rarely tell them everything. You need to be judicious about sharing information and tell as much of the truth as you planned to advise the counterparty for that particular interaction.

We are seeing more and more unethical behavior in the world. I also believe that some people think they must lie in negotiations to get what they want. I was able to maintain my integrity throughout my career by being ethical in my negotiations. You do not have to respond to a question or you can respond with another question if you do not want to answer a question.

If you catch them in a lie or they catch you in a lie, it is very difficult, if not impossible, to regain credibility. Whatever your counterparty says should be verified and not completely trusted. When a lawyer catches someone in a lie in litigation, they ask the person under oath: "So when were you telling the truth? When you told us the first story or this current story you are telling, or are both lies?"

I have a saying about this as well. "I believe none of what I hear and half of what I see and I am not sure, which half I see, I believe." This is a bit of an overstatement but you get the message. As a point of emphasis, if you were to catch your child in a lie, could you trust what he would say the next time in a similar situation?

7. Keep your negotiating team small and manage SMEs and executives.

For more material projects, your core negotiating team should include a Lead Negotiator, a lawyer, an analyst, and a second chair negotiator/facilitator.

Bosses and SMEs may give away too much information or way too much money. Prepare them for every interaction with your counterparty and their executives. Even if you prepare them, they may do something you will regret.

The Call Option

One time, we were in a meeting with a project's co-owner, including the respective presidents of each company. I was advising the attendees that the project had many problems and needed additional investment in order to run properly. While I was not involved in the initial investment decision, I was brought into the project to determine what could be done to fix the asset. I ran through the analysis to indicate the state of the project.

The president of each company had met previously to finalize the agreement to fund the project. The final agreement gave us the option to buy an additional interest from the co-owner ("Call Option"). The co-owner wanted us to exercise the Call Option to take an additional ownership interest in the project. With the project needing additional funding, it was clear in the meeting that we were not going to purchase an additional interest. Needless to say, the co-owner was not happy about the state of the project or their ownership interest. We both probably would have been better off not doing the project for various reasons, including cost.

Generally, project owners believe at funding that a project will be successful. Hence, the co-owner's president was good with giving us a Call Option to get the project funded and may not have understood the downside. Conversely, our company's president was able to include the Call Option in the agreement, mitigating our downside risk and giving us potential upside.

Regardless, you need to educate your team (including any executives and Subject Matter Experts) on what their role is in any meeting.

8. Focus on the issues, not the personality.

Focus on getting to agreement. Do not attack the personality of your counterparty. If your counterparty decides that they want to yell, let them. Do not escalate and start yelling back. Yelling at them generally does not work when they are yelling at you.

Do Not Yell When All Else Fails

I have several examples where the other party's poor behavior worked against them.

On one occasion, I was negotiating an agreement when my counterparty's Lead was on the phone. I was in the room with my lawyers and the rest of his team. We got to a point in the contract when I told him that we could not live with the change they had made to the contract. He then started yelling. He told me that we would have to revert back to the old terms in the agreement. I then told him in my calmest voice that we could not live with that either. He proceeded to yell for a while longer. Ultimately, I just said, "Let me think about the issue and we will come up with a proposal."

I let him vent and he knew that we were not going to get anywhere on the issue, so he relented. We then moved on to the next issue. It was also acceptable in that culture to yell at your counterparty and then be friends after the negotiations were over. Remember this is business and not personal. When I ran into him a few years later, he gave me a big hug.

Don't P on Me

On another occasion, upon closing of sale of a business, I was the project manager responsible for making sure that all the assets were transitioned to the new owner. I was also responsible for interim services needed during the transition period. In order to provide any services after the closing of the main sales contract, several ancillary agreements needed to be negotiated. This allowed for the services or other activities to be performed post-closing.

There was an intellectual property (IP) service contract we were negotiating with a Fortune 100 company. The IP lawyers were both quite good on both sides but could not agree on the key issues in the contract. In fact, every time the IP lawyers met, it was like an atomic bomb going off over the phone. Therefore, I asked our lead commercial negotiator if he would be the Lead Negotiator. I also asked our IP lawyer to brief the lead commercial negotiator on all the various issues in the IP contract.

We then met with the counterparty. They were expecting our IP lawyer to lead the negotiation. I think they were pleasantly surprised when we had the lead commercial negotiator as the Lead on the IP contract. We therefore made progress until we hit part of the contract regarding anti-trust provisions. It then became a free-for-all because we were all on separate phone lines in different locations. There were probably seven people on the phone talking at once. I stated in very loud voice over the phone that, "This contract is not a condition to close," which it was not.

However, their lawyer said that I was acting in "bad faith." I was absolutely quiet on the phone and did not say a word at that point. My lawyer chimed in, stating that, "I was just stating a fact." The parties had agreed that the IP contract was not a condition to close the main deal.

Unfortunately for their lawyer, she did not know I was also the transition facilitator and project manager. I had been working directly with the counterparty's lead commercial negotiator, who was also on the phone. We had developed a very credible relationship. I had already met with their outside auditors and lead commercial negotiator to discuss goodwill and a number of issues with the transition.

At this point, I negotiated the rest of the key terms of the IP contract, except for the anti-trust provision that was tabled for a later discussion. The counterparty's Lead Negotiator conceded every issue from then on, overruling any argument by his lawyer.

We found out later that the counterparty was right about the antitrust provision and we revised the contract accordingly. The counterparty should have just tabled the issue (i.e., parked it for later) instead of attacking me. They would have had more power to negotiate the rest of the terms on the IP agreement that day. The counterparty's lawyer, in this case, undermined the rest of their positions on that contract by attacking my credibility.

I cannot emphasize this enough: be soft on the people during negotiations and attack the issues. If you attack the people, there is a high probability that you will be the one that gets burned. However, you need to hold people accountable. Be careful in doing so.

9. Place risk on the party best able to control the risk or get paid to accept the risk.

For more complicated transactions, maintain a risk register. A risk register is very useful to better understand the risks you are accepting and to develop risk mitigation strategies around the risks you are accepting as part of the agreement. Capital project teams are used to maintaining these documents. Ask them for help if you need assistance. Your counterparty will try to get you to assume a risk without paying you to accept the risk. It is important to understand the risks that you are taking and those of your counterparty.

Do Not Use Their Escalator

I remember a negotiation where the counterparty was telling us that they would like a particular escalator for their cost included in the contract. After further research, we discovered that the counterparty had some control over that escalator. Needless to say, it is very important that you do your research on whatever your counterparty is asking if you do not understand the ramifications. It is also important to make sure that you use the most appropriate escalator if you agree to escalate price. If you agree to an escalator, you should also include provisions to revisit the escalator if the price moves beyond the comparable market price.

Make Them Pay

Another time the counterparty asked us to accept all environmental risks on a particular asset when they owned 50% of the asset and we owned the other 50% of the asset. The counterparty was legally responsible for their half of all costs associated with any environmental problems on that particular property. However, as operator of the property, we knew there were not a lot of environmental risks associated with the property, but we required the counterparty to pay a significant cost for us to assume that environmental risk.

Make sure that the party best able to control these risks is held responsible for costs associated with that risk in the contract or you are paid to accept the risks.

10. Never immediately accept the other side's opening offer. (And be careful changing a previously agreed clause.)

Opening offers are an interesting conundrum because project managers and executives are generally schedule driven. They want negotiations over quickly so they can move on to the next deal. The negotiator's job is to negotiate the best transaction and, most of the time, they have nothing to do with operating the asset once purchased or constructed. Additionally, when your contract is a part of a larger project, project managers and executives may not consider your contract material and may push you to finish your negotiation early.

Develop negotiation strategies for interaction with project managers and executives, as they may want you to accept the opening offer if it is close to acceptable. With project managers and executives, trust is earned but not necessarily given. Generally, everyone should do the proper negotiation planning regardless of whether it is an internal or external negotiation.

For instance, you receive an opening offer from the counterparty that is everything you ever wanted and everything you will ever need. Should you accept?

You must ask for more. Otherwise *your counterparty will have regrets if you accept immediately.* This is also called seller's remorse.

The Reluctant Buyer

To give you an example, I was teaching a class in London. I received a text from my son saying he wanted to sell his iPod for $150. However, he was chatting with a bunch of people online and offered the iPod for sale for $125. Someone in the chat room immediately accepted his offer. Legally, it was an offer and acceptance and was a binding agreement. However, in small transactions, the law does not necessarily work that way since you are not going to waste your time suing to get the iPod. My son decided that his response would be, "I need to ask my dad to see if I can sell my iPod." I received the text message stating he wanted to sell the iPod for $150. He told me how the person immediately accepted and he thought he could get more. He had seller's remorse.

I told him that he had a contract with the other party to sell it for $125. I also told him he might lose the deal if he changed the price at this point. However, he was focused on getting more money for his iPod.

My son chatted with the buyer the next day indicating that he had talked to his dad. His dad would let him sell the iPod for $150. The buyer responded that he would pay the $150 but not a penny more. The next day the buyer responded that he no longer wanted the iPod. My son still has that iPod many years later.

The lesson here is: be careful about changing the terms that have been agreed to previously. Verbal agreements are generally binding if you have an offer and acceptance. Certainly, there are a number of instances when verbal agreements are not binding and the law requires the agreement to be in writing, just not in this case. Generally, as the above example indicates, you do not want to open a previously agreed issue.

You must agree during the negotiation that you want to keep the issue open for later discussion since there are other issues that need to be discussed or for some other reason.

At the beginning of a negotiation, the parties should agree as to whether issues that have been agreed to during a negotiation are subject to reopening at any time prior to the negotiation being finalized and signed. While negotiators probably all agree that all items are negotiable until the contract is signed, in reality, the world does not necessarily work that way.

Save Face

Here is an example where, culturally, it made sense to change a previously-agreed term or condition.

We were negotiating a contract to sell a product to an Asian counterparty. We were down to one term at the end of contract negotiations that did not have a material impact on the contract value. We had to find an immaterial item to change in the contract so that we could accept the value of the last remaining item.

While this is not something intuitive to the negotiating team, I thought it was smart on the part of the manager to make sure that the negotiating team did not just give up the last remaining item in that negotiation. The negotiating team was ready to give in on the issue without looking for some other value as a tradable, which would have been a huge mistake culturally.

11. Do not negotiate against yourself.

Negotiating against yourself means making an offer after you have just made an offer instead of getting your counterparty to make a counteroffer to your offer.

In negotiating classes over the years, making another offer before getting a counteroffer is something I have seen from students over and over again. Students who do not have a lot of negotiating experience usually did this with experienced negotiators. However, in real life, this is certainly not always the case. Even experienced negotiators may be required to negotiate against themselves when it is the only way to get in the door to negotiate with the counterparty.

The Government is Not for Sale

Here is an example where negotiating against ourselves really hurt us. We were looking for land to build a project that needed a port. We went to the government requesting a plot of land for a project. We had completed a significant amount of work to advise the government on where the project should be located onshore and why. The government's response was, "No, you cannot have that piece of property ..." but they would not tell us why. The government advised us that they would sell us property further inland.

We then went back to our offices to work for two months. Our analysis proved why we needed the property just onshore instead of the property that was further from the shore. We then met with the government and showed them our work. The response from the government was, "We will sell you the property that is further from the shore. You cannot have the property adjacent to the shoreline."

During my discussions with the negotiators dealing with the state government, I thought that our project paid much fewer state taxes than other industries. I advised that the government was probably willing to hold on to the property longer to get what it wanted in state and local taxes. Therefore, continuing to try to get the property was an unwinnable battle. We realized that no deal would ever occur as the time was not right for an agreement to occur. With a deadline to get the property fast approaching, it was better to stop negotiating and move on. Hence, that project was moved to another location because the government was really saying no.

Sometimes it is best to move on to the next deal but understanding when to move on is always the issue.

12. Trust by verifying.

When I first put together my negotiation interaction rules, I had this as trust "but" verify. My co-counsel told me: trust "by" verifying. In other words, do not trust *unless* you verify. Many negotiators like to stretch the truth, not tell the whole truth, or just outright lie. As previously mentioned, puffery is one thing but lying is another that destroys your credibility; just do not do it.

We see people stretch the truth in politics, headlines, resumes, advertising, on the Internet, and certainly in negotiations all the time. I have become a cynic when it comes to getting reliable information from my counterparties.

When I am in negotiations, I seek out subject matter experts in my company or people that I trust to help me better understand why a counterparty would need or want something. It is better to research your information during the planning stage instead of waiting until face-to-face negotiations occur. You may not have a lot of time during the negotiations to do a lot of research to verify something said during your discussions. However, it is also understood you may not be able to anticipate the needs of your counterparties and will need to take a longer break to research or prepare for a new issue or circumstance.

Most commercial negotiators are not diligent enough to better understand the needs of their counterparty until face-to-face negotiations occur. You will have an advantage if you do your homework. They will miss something you understand is valuable to them.

13. Everything is negotiable.

The old adage that everything is negotiable is generally true. However, there are many reasons why a third party will not give you what you want during negotiations. These include (but are not limited) to:

- ◆ Technical,
- ◆ Alternate deadlines,
- ◆ Too valuable,
- ◆ They have alternatives,
- ◆ Lack of preparation,
- ◆ Lack of authority,

- No zone of agreement on the issue,
- Inability to meet deadlines for delivery,
- Wanting to win on every issue,
- Bottom lines, and
- Misunderstandings.

Most negotiations start out with each party trying to persuade the other of its particular position or positions. We may do this by sharing information as to what our needs and wants are, hopefully in a judicious manner. At some point, we get in a situation on an issue we want that the counterparty is unwilling to give. In this case, we need to make concessions to get what we want.

You need to find out *why* your counterparty is unwilling to negotiate on that particular issue or make concessions of similar value to get what you want. This is especially true if this is a very important issue to you or your company.

As we discussed previously, underlying interests are a big driver of all party's positions. This gets to the heart of issues that do not appear to be negotiable but in fact are.

It is important to understand that when your counterparty does not want to give you something even if you are willing to pay for it, there is a reason. Find out why and continue to negotiate. There may be a satisfactory solution to allow all parties to win.

14. Always have a plan for every interaction with your counterparty.

I have been saying for many years, "Every interaction with a third-party is a negotiation in some form." This can include trying to persuade the counterparty of your position, sharing information, getting something from the other party, or developing a relationship in some form.

Usually negotiators go to a face-to-face meeting without having done sufficient preparation to better understand the issues that will be addressed. Regardless of whether it is a short meeting or a full-blown negotiation, prepare for what will be discussed. Understand who will be at the meeting to avoid surprises.

During your career you will attend many meetings with others where they did not have a solid agenda, objectives for the meeting, action plans from the meeting, or understand who really needed to attend. This is the story of many careers. I used to facilitate the facilitator and meeting lead when I ran into these circumstances. However, that skill comes from understanding how to facilitate difficult people. You will learn facilitation of difficult people as you gain experience negotiating.

Questions

1. What are the rules for negotiation interactions?

2. Why would you only want one Lead Negotiator?

3. What is a pre-meeting with your negotiating team and why would you want to have a pre-meeting?

4. Why would you want to have an information-sharing meeting instead of negotiating issues?

5. What is a concession?

6. Why would you want face-to-face meetings instead of telephone negotiations?

7. What is ethical negotiation?

8. Why would you want a small negotiating team in your interactions with your counterparty?

9. Why would you want your counterparty to have a large negotiating team in your interactions with your team?

10. Why would you not want to respond in kind when your counterparty is acting unreasonable or yelling?

11. Why would you want to make a counteroffer to a very acceptable opening offer?

12. What is meant by negotiating against yourself?

11

Key Negotiation Tactics

This chapter covers the various negotiation tactics that will get the best results in your business or personal negotiations. If you have been successful using other tactics, by all means continue to use them. However, adding these tactics to your negotiation tool box should enable you to become even more successful.

Using tactics is more about using psychology to your advantage and understanding when your counterparty is trying to take advantage of you by using tactics. There is an undercurrent of psychological aspects to all negotiations. You will be advantaged by understanding why people do the things they do. I attempt to explain some of the reasoning behind these tactics to help you better understand when to use them.

Marketing and advertising companies have been studying us for years and understand our psychological make up very well. To name a few, Amazon and Google understand our buying and search habits extremely well. They tell us they accumulate data so they can provide more relevant products and services. At the same time, they know us better than we know ourselves. They use tactics to get you to click on more products and services you want. Whether you need them is a different issue.

Before we get to the tactics, one caveat is: be careful to not over use a tactic. It will become less and less effective with overuse in a singular negotiation. I remember that in one class I taught, a team nicknamed one of the negotiators on the other team "Nestle Crunch" since he used the tactic over and over again. You will understand the Crunch tactic better after you read the chapter.

1. Set anchors.

Anchoring is a common bias of relying too heavily on information you receive or have received even if the information is unrelated to the decision.

When I say set *anchors*, try to make offers so that your counterparty relies on your offer, statement, or data when making a counteroffer on an issue. While it is stressful making the opening offer, it can also set the bar for your counterparty to make a counteroffer to your proposal.

Researching this issue, I found a Harvard Business Review issue from 2005 called "How Strategists Really Think: Tapping the Power of Analogy" by Giovanni Gavetti and Jan Rivkin.[11] The focus of the article is on understanding our reasoning processes. The key issue is that most people do not understand that they make decisions by thinking about what happened to others or themselves in the past. While this method of decision making in negotiation may be effective since we are drawing on experience, we are also drawing on biases. This can also lead to bad decisions if we rely on incorrect or misleading information.

My favorite example of a failed analogy, which I have used in my classes for years, is from a study by Nobel Prize winner Daniel Kahneman in collaboration with Amos Tversky.[12] These researchers set up a roulette wheel to stop on either ten or sixty five. They asked the participants in the study to estimate the percent of African countries in the United Nations. The subjects that saw ten after spinning the roulette wheel estimated the percentage to be 25% on average. The subjects that saw sixty five after spinning the roulette wheel estimated the percentage to be 45% on average (or about 80% higher). The roulette wheel results had nothing to do with the composition of United Nations, but there was an obvious bias in estimating by the subjects in the study.

---

11   https://hbr.org/2005/04/how-strategists-really-think-tapping-the-power-of-analogy.

12   Kahneman, Daniel, *Thinking, Fast and Slow*, Farrar, Straus & Giroux, 2011.

There are a few other studies, including one by Dan Ariely[13], which had similar results. In Ariely's study, the subjects were told to write down the last two digits of their national IDs (social security numbers in the United States) as a potential price for various wines and chocolates. They were then asked if they would pay the amount written or the last two digits of their social security number as the price. The participants with the higher last two digits of their social security number generally agreed to pay about a 65% higher price for the same products than those participants with lower last two digits of their social security numbers. It shows that even totally unrelated numbers or information can affect your negotiations. This makes it all the more important to understand if you are being biased by your counterparty and to attempt to bias your counterparty towards your proposals.

In many places around the world, prices are marked on goods for sale. This is a form of anchoring. Everything is really negotiable, but most will not negotiate if there is a price marked on the goods for sale. Also, I look at it as how much effort should I put forth to negotiate a head of lettuce. I would probably have to talk to the store manager to be able to get a better price. The store manager would probably laugh me out of the store unless I was in India, Nigeria, or someplace where negotiating the price for your food is normal.

If I am buying a higher priced item at any store in a developed country like the United States, I try to seek out someone that I can actually negotiate the price with instead of shopping around. At major stores like Lowes or Home Depot, this is the store manager, since most employees do not have negotiation authority or in certain cases a discount may affect the employee's bonus. I negotiated for other free items when I bought a machine from Lowes but I had to negotiate with the store manager.

It never hurts to ask about reductions in price or their ability to throw something else into the purchase for free or at a reduced price.

13 Ariely, Dan, *Predictably Irrational,* HarperCollins, 2008.

The bottom line is you must understand that you may be anchored in many ways to your counterparty's price, issue, or way of thinking. Recognize it and mitigate against it! Use anchoring as a tool.

2. Crunch

Crunch is the way you respond to an unreasonable offer or to an offer you do not want to consider. When you *Crunch* your counterparty in a negotiation, you are telling them by your words or actions that their offer is not accepted as a starting point in the negotiation for those particular terms or conditions. In other words, you are expecting another offer since their offer is too unreasonable. A Crunch is also a way to try to get the counterparty to make another offer and undermine their confidence in the offer.

In most cases, the person making the offer tends to believe their offer is reasonable. I give Jim Thomas credit for coming up with the term, *Crunch*, but I am not sure where it originated. It is okay to make aggressive offers, but you need to reject unreasonable offers. Sometimes it is hard to tell the difference. If you counter an unreasonable offer instead of rejecting the offer, you have validated the offer as reasonable with your counterparty. The counterparty is free to counter your offer or try to get you to make another offer. In some cases, it is imperative that you reject the offer openly and clearly. In other cases, there may be a need to counter even when the offer is very unreasonable. Let me explain.

The Reluctant Government

We were dealing with the government on a project and they would not give us a concession. The government merely told us that our offer was not good enough to consider. In this rare case, in order to stay in play, we had to go back to our offices and work on a new proposal that hopefully met the needs of the government.

Governments are not required to tell you why they rejected your offer. You will need to try again if you want the deal. Sometimes the government is really telling us no, but we generally do not like taking no for an answer. Some executives I have worked for had this syndrome; I call it failure to listen. I also know of companies that think a bad deal gets them in the door. They think they can improve the deal later. Generally, this method of negotiations does not work, especially when dealing with governments. The Iraq oil and gas deals are a prime example of non-negotiable deals after the Gulf war.

The Impaired Listener

From a prior example, we were told no when we were trying to negotiate for land onshore for a project. The government would not tell us why it would not grant us the land. They just stated that we could have land for our project further inland. They effectively Crunched us. We still kept coming back asking for the property several times. We thought they eventually would sell us the land. Ultimately, the answer was we were not going to get the land. We needed an alternative site. Sometimes you do not know whether a Crunch means "no" or make me a reasonable offer.

There are a number of ways to Crunch. It is different in different cultures. The Japanese have a way to say make me a better offer by making a sucking sound with clinched teeth to reject your offer. Once you negotiate in any culture, you will better understand their customs including how they might Crunch you.

Some of the ways I have used Crunch on my counterparty include:

- If we agree to that issue, then our project is not financeable and is dead,
- You are going to have to do much better than that,
- Saying nothing and just look at them,
- Saying if you want that, it is going to make the project way too expensive,
- Question their logic in coming up with the offer,
- Tell them you have much better offers (be careful if you are bluffing), and
- Ask for a better offer in order to open discussions.

The Desperate Contractor

One example I would like to share with you is negotiating with a general contractor on my house. In my neighborhood a few years ago, they were repaving the roads and an offer was sent out to pave the driveways in the neighborhood. My driveway had cracks all up and down. The cost by the contractor as quoted was $5/square foot to remove and replace the existing concrete driveway. My driveway is also quite large compared to many of my neighbor's.

When the contractor arrived at my door, I told him that it might be too expensive to replace my driveway at $5/square foot. My driveway is large and it would be too expensive. As we walked out to the driveway I said, "see how large it is, I suspect it will be too expensive." He immediately stated that he could do the driveway for $4.50/square foot. I let him measure the driveway. I had already measured it and calculated the square footage and cost. He did the same calculations.

He made another offer to do the work for $4/square foot and his crew could start on Tuesday. It is always a concern when the other party knows you need the work or you are a bit desperate. Saying he could start Tuesday indicated he needed the work. This was Friday, so I told him to let me think about it until tomorrow. I would let him know.

I called the next day and asked if he could do any better on cost to replace the driveway. He came down a bit more on his price and completed the work. I actually Crunched the contractor three times without ever making a counteroffer.

I have told this story more than a few times in my negotiation classes. Invariably, students tell me that the contractor probably cut corners since I got such a good price. My response is firstly, he needed to keep his workers busy since he would start on the following Tuesday. Secondly, he was doing all the driveways in the neighborhood. He needed to maintain his reputation. I was very satisfied with the outcome and so was the contractor. He did the work. I paid him and he moved on to his next job.

3. Use silence as a weapon.

Using silence as a weapon is my favorite and most effective tactic. If you are from a country known not to use this tactic (like the USA), they may underestimate you.

My question for you is, "Can you remain silent for a substantial length of time?" You may need to do this during phone, face-to-face, or online discussions. Do you have the need to interrupt the speaker?

Good negotiators have the ability to remain silent when needed. This is true even when there is substantial pressure for the negotiator to speak. Your and your team's silence allows you to get a lot more information from your counterparty than you otherwise would. This is a learned behavior. You need to practice being silent in discussions (especially if you are an extrovert). However, do not practice on your spouse or significant other.

I have successfully used silence in my negotiations and have seen others use it effecively as well. A good example of this happened when we asked our joint venture partner to meet with us on a project.

The Lying Partner

The scenario went like this. We were sitting in our conference room talking and in walked our counterparty, our joint venture partner. The counterparty's senior management was meeting with us to discuss the project. After introductions, the commercial coordinator for the project jumped right in. He asked the counterparty how they could supply natural gas to our project. He did not see how they could meet the timeline that they were telling us. The commercial coordinator then sat there quietly for a moment or two.

Being the extrovert that he is, he could not keep himself from talking. Our commercial coordinator then proceeded again to ask how the counterparty could supply natural gas to a project when we could not see how it was possible. He went on and on about how the pipelines needed to be built. We could not build the pipelines in time to deliver the gas as timely.

Our commercial coordinator sat there quietly for a few moments. By this time he was sitting forward in his chair. His boss, our commercial manager, was sitting next to him and kicked him when he started talking again. The commercial manager had heard enough at this point.

The meeting got deathly quiet because the counterparty did not respond. All sat quietly as the counterparty grew more and more embarrassed. Finally, the counterparty's senior manager stated, "I think my team needs to step outside for a few minutes and chat." They got up, went outside, and left the building.

It became evident that whoever negotiated the delivery of gas from this counterparty had very weak penalties for not delivering the gas. Also, the counterparty had other competing projects they were working. They wanted potentially to delay or kill our project.

The counterparty leaving the building certainly validated what the commercial coordinator was saying. The quiet time actually punctuated the message. Being silence seems to be quite useful when you find the counterparty is not being honest with you.

Using silence as a technique can backfire on you if the counterparty uses the same technique. You can find yourself staring at each other in silence and accomplishing nothing. Sometimes this is best if it is a material issue that you need. If this happens, you may have little choice but to adjourn the meeting to a later date or sit until someone speaks. I have heard that whoever speaks first loses. However, asking questions is probably good in these circumstances. Sometimes deadlock on an issue may be due to miscommunication.

My students and former co-workers all have noted that being quiet has helped them in arguments with their counterparties. This is especially true in some developed nations where they are used to back and forth discussion in negotiations. The Japanese are very adept at using silence as a weapon, so it may not work as well in Asia.

I strongly recommend including this tactic in your port-folio of tools. Being silent instead of responding will benefit you many times over.

4. Practice patience and persistence.

With most of our business activities, we have deadlines. Your company will probably have deadlines and your counterparty will probably have deadlines. However, it is essential that you practice patience and persistence in negotiations. This is especially true in dealing with governments and governmental companies, which may not have deadlines or may have tax burdens they want to satisfy.

While I have seldom had problems with negotiators fail-ing to show up, many African government negotiators like to meet in more exotic locations. Therefore, many of our negotia-tions have taken place in Europe when we are dealing with African governments and companies. If you set a meeting in their native country at their office, sometimes your coun-terparty may not be available, may fail to show up, or may be constantly interrupted. This may be a message they are sending to you that they would like to meet outside of their country. I strongly suspect they like to go shopping or on va-cation in addition to meeting with you. *Understand the U.S. Foreign Corrupt Practices Act (FCPA) or other laws dealing with meetings with government officials.*

The Patient that Survived

A good example of using patience and persistence was when we were negotiating with the third-party who had access to a very similar one-sided contract we had signed, not in our favor. The contract was a public record at the Securities and Exchange Commission (SEC) in the United States. The counterparty to that contract with our company was a small, public entity. Generally, small public companies must file records with the SEC if a contract is significant to the company being a going concern, which was the case with this agreement.

Our negotiating team went to meet with the third-party, who had a copy of the one-sided contract in hand. As expected, this third-party stated they would be happy to have that contract without further negotiation. (Just to be clear, I had nothing to do with the one-sided contract. In fact, I tried to stop it.) My number one *personal* rule in life is "you cannot save people from themselves if they do not let you."

This time, the negotiating team asked for my help. I was going to do everything I could to help with negotiating a much better agreement. In this instance, we were able to mitigate the impact of the other contract we had signed. Our negotiators were very prepared. They patiently and persistently explained that contract was negotiated in a different time with different risk metrics. Our negotiators and the third-party then proceeded to go through the entire contract. More reasonable terms that fit the current investment environment were negotiated. Initially, the commercial group was panicked about what might happen in these negotiations.

Our Lead Negotiator did a fantastic job of recovering and making a good deal out of a potentially bad one. I have great respect for her abilities even though she questioned her own abilities at the time. She did a remarkable job of planning and engaging the counterparty to get what we wanted.

5. Understand biases.

Everyone has biases. You are included in that list! These may be subconscious or conscious biases. Biases affect most of the decisions we make. Understanding our biases and those of our counterparty's will help us to get better solutions and better contracts.

If your counterparty's biases are inherently repugnant to your core values, this is something you need to know. You may not want to spend a lot of time cultivating a relationship and agreement with a party with whom you do not want to do business.

Biases come in many forms, including from our culture, our experiences, parents, siblings, friends, values, others, and even before birth (instinctual).

There are many biases that affect negotiations. Wikipedia has an expansive list of many biases that is almost overwhelming. Here are a few of our more key biases affecting negotiations:

♦ *Anchoring* bias is a tendency to rely heavily or anchor on a trait or piece of information when making decisions. I have covered this in some detail already since it is very important.

♦ *Confirmation* bias is where you tend to focus on information that confirms your preconceptions and ignore other contradicting information.

♦ *Framing effect* bias is when people draw different conclusions from looking at the same information.

♦ *Information* bias, or what I affectionately call analysis paralysis, is when we continue to seek additional information that will not affect our actions or decisions.

I could talk about biases all day and give many examples. In the United States, we see biases in many forms concerning issues with gun control, abortion, healthcare, trade, drugs, immigration, defense, and government spending.

As an exercise, I want you to think about something you strongly believe (which is an inherent bias). Argue or at least think about the other side of the issue. What are their arguments against what you believe and why?

It is not my purpose to change your position on the issue. You must understand what the other party might be thinking. This will help you come to creative solutions on an issue instead of ending in a stalemate on an agreement. You will need to do this in your negotiation preparation and planning in order to counter their arguments.

You need to be careful not to empathize with the counterparty or put yourself in their position on the issues during the negotiation. There have been studies that indicate you will give away too much since our emotions tend to take over. I have said many times, "Emotions get in the way of decision quality." Check them at the door.

Another way to say this is, "Passion trumps reason." While I am passionate in my negotiations, I am not afraid to make a concession to get a reasonable solution.

The key here is to recognize your biases and mitigate their effect on you and your team. Alternatively, try to use your counterparty's biases to your advantage.

6. Use power.

Power comes in many forms, including age, experience, personal knowledge, BATNA (best alternative to the negotiated agreement), patience, persistence, legal support, skill, key consultants, subject matter experts, relationships, reputation, and homework.

When Managers Collide

Sometimes is it better not to display your power. One time I had two senior managers that were extremely upset about a particular issue. One manager issued a memo that required all the other senior managers to follow "required guidance" without consulting the managers that actually worked on this issue.

Needless to say, one senior manager told me he was going to disrupt a senior manager's meeting. He was going to potentially embarrass the other senior manager in front of his co-workers. When I heard this, I knew that we would only get to disagreement. Both senior managers had quite a bit of power, but it was somewhat equal in the company.

I went to one of the senior managers that created the problem. I advised him that the other senior manager was going to disrupt an important meeting coming up. His initial response was he was going to stick to the agenda and kick the issue out of the meeting. I recommended a separate face-to-face meeting so the other senior manager could advise what his thinking was on this issue in a safe environment for both of them. I did the same impression with the other senior manager.

The senior managers met and agreed on a path forward. Both were subsequently promoted to more important roles, not that I had anything to do with their promotions. I offered to teach all of our senior managers negotiation skills. Sad to say, they turned me down.

My story focuses on using your power wisely. Whatever power you do have, plan to use it when it makes sense. Hide your power when it will hurt you.

Sometimes you may not have power, but you can create competition where there is none. This gives you power. Having alternatives can create a lot of power even if it is an illusion. In this case, your counterparty must believe you have alternatives. This is also referred to as having BATNAs.

The Power Play

In another example, we were selling a business. When we went out to bid for the asset using an offering memorandum, the parties came back with indicative offers. There were only a few potential purchasers for the business. All of the offers we received were terrible except one. However, we kept all the parties in play during visits to the data room. We wanted to make sure that the one party that had a mostly acceptable bid knew that there was competition.

Our plan worked. We received final offers from all the parties, which were similar to their original offers. We negotiated the final agreement, selling the business to the party we expected to buy the business.

We were hopeful the other bidders might increase their offers. However, they really were never in the running to buy the business since it would have been a substantial increase to get to the best offer. Here, we created competition by keeping all the parties in play and not eliminating unreasonable offers. It also made sure the best offer had some pressure to negotiate a fair agreement.

It is very important to understand you and your counterparty's power that might affect your negotiations. When I originally taught negotiations, one of my subject matter experts that helped me create the course told me power is very important. He told me I should spend more time developing this really important point in my class. I have come to believe he was correct.

To help you with power issues on larger business deals, I suggest you create and maintain a stakeholder management plan, included in the framing tool in the Appendix. The stakeholder management plan should list key stakeholders, their potential impact on your negotiations, what they support, and details any mitigation plans. By understanding those with power, you may be able to contain problems before they arise.

7. Create and maintain competition.

I have been told to get at least three bids from contractors to make them compete against each other. I suspect you have heard the same. While I do not always do this, getting competing bids has come in handy on a few occasions where competition really did not exist or was tentative.

The Clueless Bidder

In a similar situation to the above example under power, we received several offers for a technology business. However, only one of the offers was close to acceptable. However, we treated all the bidders as if they were important and made valid bids. We invited all of the bidders into the data rooms and set up a timeline to receive a binding offer from all the bidders.

There was one particular bidder that thought they were too important to go through the process. They told us that one week was not enough time to go through the data room. They told us they needed the data room the next week. In good form, I looked them in the eye and said," Well, that is going to be a problem since we have other people in the data room next week." I would look at the timelines for other bidders and put them back in the data room when the other bidders had finished their turns. I could see the surprise in their eyes when they realized they were not the only bidder coming to the data room. Ironically, the people who wanted the extra days in the data room had not made that great an offer compared with the others anyway.

Even if you do not plan for it, there are many opportunities for negotiation tactics. I never let the other party see fear in my eyes. In fact, I was looking for it in their eyes with my response and I got it. It pays to think on your feet since you will be surprised many times during your negotiations.

Since the best bidder went through the data room first, we went ahead and entered into negotiations since they provided another offer post data room. Do not think you have to wait until your timelines are met to begin negotiations with the best offer. This is especially true if that is the best offer you think you will get. Try to make sure the others are not aware of what you are doing since they may want to enter into negotiations or decide not to make an offer. Having the other bidders in play can give you leverage when you negotiate with the best bidder.

8. Focus on and create small wins early for both parties.

Focus on small wins early in the negotiation if there are big issues that you need to have some cooperation to get a resolution. This tends to create good will on both sides of the negotiations. The parties see that progress is being made. These big issues might be complicated or they may be issues that will stop your project from going forward.

The Clueless Project Manager

For example, in a conference call with the counterparty, on our side of a phone negotiation there was a project manager, a commercial coordinator, local lawyer, and myself. Our counterparty had probably five or six people on the line on the phone, including their lawyer and their lead commercial negotiator. This was my first meeting on the negotiation. The parties had been negotiating for many months. We had several different Lead Negotiators on our side of the table over that time. When I engaged the team, our project manager had assumed the role of the Lead Negotiator. He was yelling over the phone at the counterparty's Lead Negotiator. The Lead Negotiator for the counterparty responded in kind by yelling as well. This went on for approximately an hour or more. The parties hung up frustrated and angry with little being accomplished.

In my mind, this agreement was not going anywhere anytime soon. Frankly, the project manager had made a prior concession on an issue in a separate contract. The counterparty wanted to take back the concessions in this contract. We had little leverage to stop them. This was clearly unacceptable to the project manager. His emotions were getting the best of him. The project manager was not a trained negotiator. He did not last long as the lead.

The Clueless Lawyer

In the same negotiation two months later, I arrived in country to find the project manager had been replaced by our local legal counsel as the Lead Negotiator. Our new Lead Negotiator had invited the counterparty, including their lawyers, to our office on an extremely hot day. They had walked down the street to our offices. All the counterparty's negotiating team were wet with perspiration by the time they arrived. I continued to be an observer at this point.

This day's negotiation and discussions ended very similarly to the one two months prior. In this case, the lawyers decided to do a page turn on the contract, which is not unusual. However, on page five of a ninety-page contract, an extremely material issue started being discussed by both parties. At this point, both Lead Negotiators started yelling at each other, which is not uncommon in the host country. This set the tone for the next several hours – neither party would agree to anything as we went through the contract. I did not see agreement being something we would get anytime soon.

At the end of that day, we set a time to meet the next day. The counterparty showed up again the next day. The lawyers proceeded to do a page turn, got to page five, and the same thing happened all over again. I was a newcomer to the meeting but I had seen enough. I put my hands up into a T to call a timeout and said we were not getting anywhere with this issue. We need to skip this issue and move on to other areas, which we did. Although during the rest of the meeting neither party yelled at each other, the tone was set during the prior interactions where neither party wanted to agree to anything the other party had brought up. However, we were able to discuss some of the smaller issues and these issues in later meetings became more easily agreed to by both parties.

The Adapter

I subsequently took over as the Lead Negotiator. I focused on facilitating a discussion of the smaller issues, trying to change the tone of the negotiations. I decided to change the negotiation process drastically. Firstly, I agreed that we should meet at the counterparty's lawyer's office so they would feel more comfortable negotiating the contract. Secondarily, I requested that we negotiate using a position table so we can organize the issues better instead of a page turn of the contract, avoiding the big issue on page five for now. Lastly, I conceded that we would negotiate in the local language on issues where I was not the lead. My lawyers would be prepared to negotiate many smaller issues while I was in the room and keep me informed. We did get sidetracked a number of times on issues where I had to step in and explain to the parties why an issue was required by us, even though I was not the lead on that issue.

What this did was help the counterparty's technical SMEs better understand the contract. We finally started seeing feedback on technical issues so that all parts of the contract could be negotiated. Additionally, the behaviors of all parties improved drastically. I was the only one in the negotiations that did not speak the local language. Therefore, all the counterparty's attendees understood what was happening during the negotiations. This greatly

> improved the relationship of the counterparties. We still hit
> some roadblocks along the way but we moved past them
> to complete the key terms of the contract during the next
> several months.

Looking back, agreeing to move the negotiations to the counterparty's lawyer's office, using a position table, and negotiating local language were all small wins (or maybe big wins) for the counterparty. It changed the tone and the direction of the negotiation.

Sometimes you need to create small wins for both parties to progress a difficult negotiation. However, I would not wait to the end of the negotiations to discuss deal breaker issues. This knowledge may only come through longer term discussions with your counterparty. The sooner you know the deal breakers, the earlier you can move on to another transaction.

9. Group issues at the end of the negotiation to suggest final solutions on all key issues to close the deal.

In the negotiation in the previous section, the one contract turned into three separate contracts. As we approached the end of our negotiations of all these contracts, it became apparent to me that there were fourteen key issues in the three contracts that we continued to have differences.

The Groupie

> By this time, the parties had been discussing many of
> the key terms and conditions of these contracts for many
> months, in fact years. However, it was clear that neither
> party wanted to make a concession on any individual issue
> without discussing the other issues.
>
> Therefore, we put together a PowerPoint presentation
> on each of the key issues. We went through each issue with
> my negotiating team, discussing the position of each party.
> We then agreed what would be a solution to which each
> party could agree based on our past discussions. We met
> with our counterparty to present our solutions.
>
> As part of the process, I stated, "Because we have been
> negotiating these issues for many months, it has become

apparent what both parties were really willing to agree to but needed to come to terms on all the issues at one time. I propose the PowerPoint presentation as an overall approach to all the remaining key terms. I am going to go through all of these fourteen key issues that are on the table. I will advise what we think is a reasonable solution based on all our prior discussions for each issue. Both parties will be making concessions but my offer for a solution is on all fourteen issues. I want you to hear all the issues and judge for yourself whether you can agree to all of them, or none of them. However, I do not want to agree to some, it must be all. You are not allowed to cherry pick the ones that benefit you. It is all or nothing."

I actually did have a problem with one of the issues for which I could not come up with a reasonable solution. I saved this item for later in the presentation. After my presentation, we had a discussion of this last issue and were able to come to a reasonable solution.

We came to terms that day on all the key issues after lots of discussion on each issue.

Because I took the time during all of the negotiation to explain in detail why we needed each issue that we requested, I developed a great rapport with my counterparty. Initially, the counterparty was trying to win on every issue, which told us that they had never negotiated these types of contracts previously.

10. Leverage the power of loss aversion (group their losses).

This is a characteristic that we humans all share: we tend to dislike losses much greater than we like wins for the same amount. This sounds funny but, there have been a number of studies to prove this point. Think about your losses. How much more do your losses hurt than wins make you feel better, whether you are gambling, trading stocks, or taking a loss in life or your business?

I really did not need a group of studies to tell me this since I own stock in the stock market. It seems I am in pain when the market goes down. If the market goes up, I am happier, just not *that* happy.

Group the counterparty's losses. Conversely, keep your losses separate so you can get something for each loss.

The Groupie 2

In the prior section, we were at the end of the key negotiations. I had recommended solutions on all key issues. I presented each issue separately and explained the reasoning. This is an example of grouping our and our counterparty's losses and gains in an attempt to close out the remaining key issues. We had been negotiating for many months at this point. We also had a very good understanding of what was acceptable to both parties.

Grouping losses takes planning. This is a way to get your counterparty to take one big loss instead of several smaller losses (which would cause you to pay a higher overall price). To state this another way, your counterparty will take one loss instead of losses on several issues in exchange for one loss that you take on an issue. You do this by looking for areas where you can concurrently discuss several issues. Look for dependent issues that make sense discussing together, such as different risks and associated damages.

An example of this might be when your counterparty wants you to accept a risk that you were willing to accept. You ask in return for them to pay you to bear the cost of the risk plus have them accept additional damages if they provide the product late.

While not as beneficial, it is easier to group losses at the end of the negotiations since you have discussed all the key issues and better understand of the value of each issue. However, you will probably be consolidating your losses on several issues in order to close your agreement.

11. Understand what non-verbal communications are telling you.

Watch the body language of your counterparty at all times. This includes their facial expressions, arms waving, head nodding, and posture. Their body language can be very telling.

Watch for signs from the other side of non-verbal comments. These include putting their hand over their mouth, looking at the ceiling, rolling the eyes, looking past you when they are telling a lie or made a mistake saying something. Jan Hargrave's *Strictly Business: Body Language*,[14] is a good book on body language and can explain what each of these non-verbal actions may indicate. Jan is also an excellent speaker if you have a broader audience that needs to better understand body language. I do not plan to discuss body language issues in detail in this book since Jan is the real expert. You will learn much more from reading her book.

However, some things you should be aware of without having to read the book on body language are:

♦ Be aware of where you are supposed to sit at the table and understand local customs. This is especially important in Asia.

♦ Even though the other side is yelling, do not respond in kind (i.e., do not escalate). Try to stay calm even if you have to bite your tongue. You can say you understand how they feel. This is not agreeing, just validating their feelings, which is sometimes all you need to do to get past the issue.

♦ Talk slowly and use simple words when the language you are speaking is not their primary language. However, do not make them look foolish by talking too slow.

♦ Understand you and your counterparty's emotional intelligence. This is understanding what the impact of the parties' emotions has on the negotiations. Emotions do get in the way of good decision quality.

♦ Listen and do not respond too quickly. Repeat what you heard to verify, especially when English is not the primary language. Seek to understand and then seek to be understood.

While I am a bit biased, I believe women generally get body language clues much better than men (just ask any wife, Ginger).

---

14 Ibid.

Most communication is non-verbal. Jan Hargrave states that much as 70 to 80% of all communication is non-verbal. Therefore, it is extremely important that you learn the clues of body language and what their non-verbal statements may be saying to you.

The Signal Bearer

I have a good friend, also an excellent lawyer, who gets frustrated when he believes the other party is being very unreasonable. He puts his head in his hands briefly to show his frustration or disappointment in the counterparty. However, it is just as likely that this is his clue to one of us on his team to call for a break to get him out of the room for a little while.

It is extremely important that your team maintains their body language in a consistent manner. During one of the practice exercises in a negotiation course I was teaching, one of the teams was displaying body language indicating that they did not support what the Lead Negotiator was saying. I called a timeout during the negotiation session to have an offline discussion with the team. We discussed why they were acting that way. All internal discussions about negotiation positions should take place before the meeting with the counterparty. Once you are in the negotiation, all team members must support the Lead Negotiator both verbally and with their body language.

If an issue arises that you have not discussed as a team, stop the Lead Negotiator from negotiating, especially if the body language indicates that he or she was ready to jump in on the issue. The Lead should table or set aside the issue until discussed with the negotiating team. Sometimes people get a bit too eager.

The Body's Language

I have given you several examples in this book about using body language to your advantage, like the time I had to act out with my lawyers by yelling so that the counterparty could hear in the adjacent room. I was not happy about the counterparty being there without their Lead Negotiator just to gather information. I suspect they imagined my angry face and body language at the time even though I was not in the room. Actually, I just wanted progress on our negotiations since I had flown a long way to get to the location.

Basically, body language is when people unconsciously provide clues to what they really may be thinking. Body language is far from an exact science. It can be telling if the other party is giving off the clues or if you want to send a message.

12. Avoid making a concession larger than the one preceding it on any issue.

Have a concession plan on any key issues and stick to your plan. Key issues include those issues you believe are important to your counterparty but may have little value to you. If the other party makes an offer and it does not fit with your plan to get to a reasonable solution, you may want to revisit your counteroffer before implementing your concession plan.

Another problem that arises is you may start doubting yourself after the counterparty has made an offer that is significantly different than you expected. Focus on where you want to be at the end of the discussion of the issue. Opening offers are all over the place when it comes to you deciding on your concession plan.

The Annoying Flipper

For example, I was selling my in-laws' house for them using a power of attorney. Before I found a real estate agent, a relative suggested someone they knew as a buyer. This potential buyer wanted to make an offer before we hired a real estate agent. I certainly would accept an offer but I also discounted the value of such an offer since they were house flippers (who we'll refer to as "Flipper"). Therefore, I commissioned a local real estate appraiser to give me an idea of the fair market value for any sale. Since I am far from an expert on local real estate values, I needed a subject matter expert.

The appraiser provided a fair market value of $265,000. The Flipper's original verbal offer was $230,000, however,

I asked for the offer in writing. The Flipper then provided a $220,000 offer as-is plus closing costs. Since we were selling pre-marketing, we would avoid having to pay the six percent realtor fee. First, always get the offer in writing when selling real estate. Second, you are never required to make a counteroffer.

A couple of weeks later, I was contacted by Flipper and they wanted to explain their offer. I declined. I told them I had an appraisal and I was better off selling through a realtor since I would get more funds. I was not going to let them explain their offer and why they thought it was reasonable. Subsequently, Flipper decided to provide another written offer of $235,000 as-is plus closing costs. At this point, I decided that I was justified in making a concession and made a counteroffer of $250,000 indicating that I had met the neighbors across the street who sold their house for $90,000 more than my offer (but that included a realtor fee and they had updated some of the house). I could not see how they could justify a hundred-thousand-dollar discount on my in-law's house. At this point, we went our separate ways since Flipper would not move off their last offer.

The Patient Concession

After I listed the house with a realtor for sale at $293,000. I decided to lower the price to $287,000 the next week since I thought it was overpriced based on the list-to-sales prices in recent weeks.

After about two months on the market and receiving several offers from house flippers, I received an offer of $245,000 from a potential buyer. I decided not to make a counteroffer. Sometimes, it is best to wait to see if the buyer will make another offer, i.e., negotiate against themselves. Certainly, you do not want to come down to validate an unreasonable offer.

Subsequently, I received another offer from this buyer at $253,000. We decided to counter the offer at $273,000 and then make smaller concessions to get to focus on $268,000 as our final price prior to required inspection prior to purchase. The buyer came up to $263,000. We then countered with an offer of $268,000 subject of course to inspection and they accepted. I knew there were a number of obvious issues with the house. I would probably have to make some additional concessions but I was not going to make many.

After inspection, as expected, there were a number of issues with the house since it had never been updated and the roof needed to be replaced. This was all in the disclosure document that we provided to the buyer prior to us coming to agreement. The buyer advised in their updated offer after the inspection that we should pay to remove the deck in the back yard, replace the roof and replace the electrical panel in the garage. They subsequently lowered their price by $20,000 to $248,000.

My response was I can wait for the next buyer and did not make an initial counter. I then waited without responding. Subsequently heard from the buyer's realtor that we are supposed to make a counteroffer and negotiate. I said sorry I do not work that way. I told them we were too far apart to make a counteroffer. I advised them that all the items mentioned in their last offer were listed in the disclosure and were obviously needing replacing.

Ultimately, I did counter at $264,000 price ($1,000 below my written appraisal of the house). However, I decided to wait to make this offer since I was not in a hurry. I heard that these buyers had been looking for a house for some time. Also, my realtor was sick in the hospital so I was directly negotiating with the realtor and buyers. Once updated by the new owners doing most of the work, the house would be worth at least $70,000 more. I knew I had the right buyers. I just needed to wait for them to accept the $264,000 offer price, which they did.

The Patient Buyer

In another example but from the buyer's prospective, I helped my son buy his house outside of Austin. We had countered back and forth a couple of times with the seller to come to agreement prior to the house inspection. During the inspection we found out that the air conditioner was 20 years old and really needed replacement immediately. The seller would not reduce the price of the house to pay for a new air conditioner but offered to split the cost of the air conditioner. During our concession process, we focused on the cost that we thought was the right value after considering the key issues in the inspection.

I told my son that we should sit on the final offer from the seller and not accept their counteroffer on splitting the costs immediately. I surmised that the seller was buying another house since he was on his second marriage with kids. Additionally, they needed to sell the current house to use the funds to purchase the next house. A few days after we received their offer to split the cost of the air conditioner, the seller contacted us. The seller advised us they were willing to do what was necessary to close the deal. In other words, they were negotiating against themselves and falling into our concession strategy.

Ultimately, we received the full cost to replace the air conditioner in my son's new house. I cannot stress the need to plan your negotiations even in buying and selling a house or a car. Buying or selling a house is probably the largest personal transaction many of us do in our lifetimes.

To reiterate: have a concession plan on key issues and stick to it.

Using Tactics

There are a number of other tactics in the many negotiation books I have run across in my negotiations journey. However, I believe the twelve tactics in this chapter have added the most value in my business and personal agreements.

Questions

1. What are the key negotiation tactics?

2. What is an anchor in negotiations and why is it important?

3. What are some ways to reject an offer as invalid and what is this called?

4. Why do you think it is so difficult to remain quiet when negotiating?

5. What are some types of biases affecting negotiations?

6. Why is it important to understand your biases?

7. What are some of the forms of power and why is understanding who has power in a negotiation matter?

8. Under what circumstances would you want your counterparty to know how much power you have?

9. Under what circumstances would you want your counterparty to not know how much power you have?

10. What are some ways to maintain competition for assets you are selling in a bid round with several bidders but only one fair offer?

11. What are some ways to establish competition in a negotiation when negotiating with only one party?

12. Why would you want to group offers on several issues?

13. What should you do if your counterparty tries to group offers on several issues?

14. What is loss aversion and why is it important in negotiations?

15. Why is body language important in negotiations?

16. Why would you want to have a concession plan on key issues?

17. In what instances do you think it would be acceptable to make a larger concession on an issue that you previously made?

Exercise: Determine who has opposing biases on an issue on something controversial. Have each participant to argue for their opponents' bias with the other party.

12
Negotiation Truisms

Negotiation truisms are truths that you need to be concerned about during your negotiations. I have pointed out behaviors and needs as items of interest in this chapter. I also suspect there are other truths that you may encounter during your negotiations. These truths are some that I have encountered during my negotiation travels.

1. The moment of the opening offer is generally the most important and most stressful in the entire negotiation.

Whether you are making the opening offer or not, you probably do not know or understand the expectations of the counterparty. I am always thinking, "Should I be more aggressive to get more from the counterparty?" However, many people believe if they are too aggressive, the opening offer may kill the negotiation.

The Aggressive Insurer

When I was involved in a lawsuit with an experienced lawyer in Colorado, he told me that earlier in his career he would always get extremely upset with insurance company's tactics. The insurance industry generally makes very aggressive opening offers and waits. The Colorado lawyer learned, as I have, that receiving or giving aggressive opening offers is a normal business negotiating tactic. We ultimately had to sue the insured person to get to a reasonable settlement from the insurance company.

There are times when you are dealing with a close or long-time friend, when it makes sense to be more reasonable. You will get to agreement faster and be able to move on to the next deal. Your worst deals, however, are generally with those people closest to you.

Many of my relatives have "borrowed" money from me in the past. I am still waiting to get repaid. I have lowered my expectation of getting repaid by my relatives over the years. However, I still view the money borrowed as being owed. To put it another way, when they have not repaid me previously, it makes it much more difficult for them to borrow additional funds in the future.

2. Stress levels change behaviors.

Have you ever noticed that when you are under a lot of stress, you become more aggressive, or do you just pull back into yourself and get quiet? I do not have all the answers on this one. However, I do know that when I am under stress, I become much more aggressive and start barking orders. Since I have this tendency, I try to mitigate the impact of my behavior on others. I was asked a number of times why I seemed to be cool under fire. It took a lot of effort but I needed to be that way to help my employees get through their difficulties with other co-workers or their teams.

You must recognize that your normal business behavior may change with higher stress levels. You will need to mitigate your behavior change and the impact on others. There are instances where you might plan to change your behavior to get someone to do something differently.

I find stress is not unlike alcohol: if you are obnoxious and drink heavily, you become more obnoxious. My findings are far from scientific but I have had many interactions with people over the years in various settings.

Watch levels of stress in others to see what is happening when they are acting unusual. The consequences of not understanding stress levels and their impacts can hurt your project, team, marriage, or partnerships.

3. It is better to negotiate an issue when you have leverage.

Risk is part of the negotiation process but it needs to be measured. In some contracts, there are clauses that allow a contract to be reopened if circumstances change or may specify terms that will be negotiated later. These types of clauses can create a scenario that someone will be negotiating later with little or no leverage.

In the negotiation world, you will find that five years from when you close on an agreement, the world will have changed. Since we do not know what will happen, we try to plan in our contracts to mitigate or project what these impacts will be. If you negotiate a long-term contract, someone will look at the contract at some point and say, "What were these people thinking?"

Those that write history get to tell whatever story they want. If you want thanks for a job well done, you might want to try another profession than negotiations. You are not likely to get any thanks for negotiating a good deal. Everyone is a critic.

The Penalty Box

We were negotiating a non-binding letter of intent when the counterparty decided that they wanted to negotiate a complete contract. I agreed. However, the agreement had a penalty clause that said, "to be negotiated later" even though my predecessors had negotiated other penalty provisions already. I did not want our company to negotiate this clause later since we had little leverage later, especially with this particular company. Funny that executives rarely see it that way unless they are skilled negotiators, but that is a different issue and another story.

My counterparty's idea of the penalty was substantially different than mine and completely unreasonable for this type of agreement. I countered their offer, indicating that we had negotiated damage provisions already in the other contract and these damage provisions were unnecessary.

It took quite a bit of time to mitigate this damage clause. I probably should have taken even more time to mitigate the clause some more. However, based on the type of agreement, I surmised that we would end up renegotiating the agreement at a later date since our terms were probably a lot more favorable than the counterparty expected on price.

We did renegotiate this agreement at a later date. The counterparty was paying significantly more to purchase the product and resell to us when we ultimately needed the product. If I was wrong though, we could have been stuck with that contract for a number of years with higher penalties that I really wanted. The current solution was still a lot better than getting penalized later. The counterparty would have proposed the same extremely stiff penalties and we would have had little leverage. My concern was that management would have rolled over and taken the penalty.

4. For complicated business deals, you "need" a great, highly skilled lawyer and negotiator.

Having a great, highly skilled lawyer and negotiator is a must for complicated business deals. I have had a great internal company lawyer on some of my deals and we did great deals. Also, I have seen companies throw people into situations where they were barely competent to negotiate. We have to start somewhere, but it is best learning from the best.

The Penitentiary Lawyer

On one deal, while I thought my lawyer was good, I found out later he was going to be serving time in a United States federal penitentiary. He had committed a felony while employed by another company before he became my lawyer. I was a bit stunned when I found out. In fact, the country manager on the deal called me to tell me. I suspect my legal group was too embarrassed to tell me.

This goes back to my rule about trust but verify. People are a big issue. These issues with the lawyer's crimes came out publicly after my dealings with this lawyer. I would not have been able to catch this issue especially since my legal department hired him.

To become a great negotiator, training only does so much for negotiation skills – you need experience. Find a place to negotiate wherever you are. Find a mentor. Experience is the best teacher (but it can be a cruel master). It is best to practice your negotiating skills in a safe environment. If you are in over your head in a negotiation, you might learn the lessons after you are finished but not prior to making the mistakes.

Every interaction is a negotiation: be prepared. Just do not take yourself too seriously when dealing with your spouse or close friends.

5. Your job as negotiator of a long-term contract is to get the best, most profitable, legal deal while letting the counterparty make "some" money.

Your counterparty needs to make some money or have their needs met. This is especially true if their bankruptcy will negatively impact your project more than the value of your contract.

The Bankrupt Man

I remember a negotiator that was removed from his job because he was so aggressive. Some small companies wanted to do business with our company at all cost. Of the three contracts he negotiated on three different projects, all ultimately were in some form of work stoppage on our projects. These small companies ran out of funds since they apparently bid under their own cost.

The outcomes on each of these contracts negatively impacted all three projects associated with the contracts. The project had to pay more funds either to the contractor or a third party to make sure the activities were completed on the project.

There are a number of instances where I have seen the same thing happen on other projects including large mega-projects. Sometimes there are forces outside of control such as significant currency fluctuations that we did not consider.

6. If there is no zone of agreement on a key issue, then there is no deal.

If both parties have done their homework, both know where their own bottom lines are on the key issues. Unless there is a valid reason or executive management has released you to go below your bottom line, you must hold to the bottom line on the issues. This may kill your contract since there may be no zone of agreement on a key issue between these bottom lines.

However, you need to understand your bottom lines on key issues so that your contract and project does not destroy more value than it creates. In some instances, it might be more important to have the higher cost contract in order to have the greater project.

Conversely, there have been a number of occasions when we did not determine our bottom line. In these cases, the company probably lost money on these projects. They might not have learned of the loss unless they did a "lookback" on the project. Even then, if the lookback is not prepared by an objective source, the truth will likely be buried.

Questions

1. What are some negotiation truisms including any you think should apply as well?

2. Why would presenting an opening offer to a counter-party be stressful?

3. Why do stress levels change behaviors?

4. What behavior changes have you noticed in people in stressful situations? What was the result?

5. How can agreements reached today be unreasonable in a few years? How would you propose mitigating this issue?

6. What do I mean by "experience is the best teacher but it can be a cruel master"?

7. Why would you want your counterparty to make money in a transaction?

8. What is a zone of agreement on an issue and why it is important?

13

Employment Negotiations

Employment negotiations can be difficult regarding work assignments, promotions, ratings, and compensation regardless if you are the employed or the employer.

Seeking employment has become much more faceless and mostly completed online. This is an area I am not going to address. It is also hard to negotiate when the other party will not engage.

Let us discuss each of the three main employment categories where engagement takes place once employed.

Negotiation with Your Manager

You need to think about every interaction with your manager. These interactions affect your work, promotions, and compensation.

It is difficult to negotiate salary increases or promotions. You need some kind of leverage or success accomplishing important activities during the year. Negotiating the best type of work is a must. Generally, the work goes to the person that their manager thinks can best handle the work. Speak up to let your manager know about your work. You should let him or her know what you accomplished and how important your accomplishments were to the department and company. However, do not be surprised if your manager does not give you credit for something that you completed.

The Credit Clause

I remember I told my manager and her manager that I came up with a tax strategy that saved the company millions of dollars on a project. I was a tax specialist for part of my career so I knew the tax laws. At this time in my career, I was an analyst but was not in the tax department. My managers advised me that they would not give me credit for something that the tax department must have developed. Needless to say, the tax department took credit for my idea. Get over it and move on.

The Competitive Promotion

I have been somewhat successful in negotiating promotions. In one case, I had applied for two different jobs in the company. I had negotiated with both executives in each business unit to determine what pay I would be receiving. In the first discussion with one of the executives, he advised me that my pay would be exactly the same and I would not get a promotion. Therefore, I approached the executive from the other business unit to discuss the work.

Since information is power, I did not tell the second executive whether I would get a raise or promotion in the other business unit. However, he might have presumed I would get both. The second executive also knew me fairly well and was known as a fairly good negotiator. However, I do believe he wanted me on his team and offered me both a promotion and additional compensation. I received a call from him years later when he was a chief executive officer of another company wanting me to come to work for him since he trusted me. You will have to come up with your own story if you have more than one offer of employment. However, I had leverage since I knew both executives and they both knew my work.

The Sideways Promotion

The other promotion I negotiated was when I was somewhat dissatisfied with my current employment. I let it be known that I was looking for external employment. This approach needs to be handled with great care because you want continued employment if you do not find other employment. Your relationship with your current manager may be such that you can let them know of your dissatisfaction. I told my manager that I was interviewing with other companies and for what jobs I was interviewing for. That was the last promotion I received, which was about a decade before I retired.

You will find as you get later into your career, you will become more and more specialized and experienced. The opportunities for promotion and salary increases will lessen. There are fewer specialist and managers needed at higher levels in companies; hopefully you will be well paid for your contribution to the company.

Generally, to get the best salary increases, you need to accomplish more than your competition in your same pay grade. However, I also found this is not always true. Biases get in the way of good decision quality when it comes to compensation and promotions.

Negotiation with Your Employees

Your employees will ask you what they can do to get the highest rating at year end or get promoted. Some of your employees will not be working on the best projects and will not be able to get the best ratings. Some of your employees will want a high rating even though you have been telling them all year that was not possible. Some of your employees think they deserve better than what you are prepared to give them. What do you do?

When negotiating with your employees about work load, salary increases, or potential promotions, it is better to discuss their progress as the year progresses. Do not wait until year end. I liked to meet with all my employees and their direct reports at least once a month. I believe at a minimum, you should at least meet with your direct reports monthly to discuss their work.

Many companies want their managers to meet with their employee at the beginning of the year, mid-year, and year-end to finalize their progress. Even with training, I found that many managers barely met these parameters. Managers tend to digress in these "employee" meetings into discussions about work issues. Some managers avoid discussions of the employee's progress and potential. I also found that managers are inconsistent in holding people accountable. In many of these cases, the employee tended to be surprised by whatever the manager presents to the employee for salary or bonus.

There are all sorts of managers from the micro-manager to the manager that pays little to no attention to you all year. Some managers are great handling good performers but are poor managers when it comes to some of their more difficult people. Handling difficult employees is an art that even human resources has difficulty helping managers handle. Handle employees (including difficult employees) directly and do not let the problem fester. Much of the time in larger companies, problem employees are passed on to other managers instead of taking corrective action. This is probably because handing under-performing employees is time consuming, difficult, and is sometimes depressing.

Besides meeting with my employees throughout the year discussing their progress, I asked my employees to draft a letter outlining their top three to five accomplishments for the year. These accomplishments should be in line with the objectives set out at the beginning of the year and updated mid-year. I spent the time to rewrite each submitted list in a form that best sold their accomplishments. I also included my version of their key accomplishments on the employee's performance agreement.

I used my employee's accomplishments versus other employees' accomplishments at the same paygrade to get the best outcomes for my employees regarding promotions and compensation. I was quite successful at getting what I wanted when we were competing with other departments. In fact, I was attacked one year by another manager who thought I was cheating somehow. The next year the business unit changed the ranking system. Preparing and being prepared to present this information in ranking sessions in companies is one of the most important parts of the manager's job.

Every company is different. You may not have the chance to argue for your employees. However, it is important to document your employees' accomplishments for employee ranking sessions. As a manager or executive, you are always negotiating with your employees in some capacity about their work and compensation; prepare as best you can.

Negotiation with Managers and Executives

I touched on negotiating with other managers in the prior section regarding your employees' rankings and salary discussions.

The Known Managers

I also gave an example earlier in the book where two executives were arguing over corporate guidance. One manager did not like the corporate guidance. He knew that there were mitigating circumstances that negated the new guidance. This executive was going to disrupt the other manager's meeting to start an argument over the new guidance. I interceded between the two, acting as mediator, bringing them together separately to get to a positive outcome. However, I knew both managers.

Negotiating with your company executives and managers whom you do not know is career limiting. I have not generally been successful at doing this. I have tried different unsuccessful approaches. I gave you an example earlier in the book where an executive thought that a project must move forward regardless of the consequences since it might affect a much larger project. Unless you know the executive and can have a candid one-on-one conversation with the executive, there is very little chance of changing their mind.

The Stubborn Executive

I tried unsuccessfully to stop an uneconomic project that an executive thought he wanted. In this case, even the people I knew that talked to this executive said the project I tried to stop was a "dime waiting on a dollar." The project destroyed about 1% of the value of the company. When an executive makes up his or her mind, it is time to move on. I like the saying, "You cannot save people from themselves if they will not let you."

Be thoughtful when negotiating with managers and executives above your paygrade. The rule, praise in public and criticize in private applies in general but especially applies to executives. Many executives have big egos and will criticize you in a public setting for offering advice unless you are asked to provide advice. However, if you know the executive and can have a one-on-one conversation with the executive, you might be able change their mind on an issue. One of the strengths of decision analysis is that alternatives and potential ranges of outcomes are presented to the executive(s), but the decision is left for the executive to make.

In salary discussions about employees, there will be an inherent bias against an employee when your manager or other managers had a negative outcome with that employee, however small. This could be from a brief interaction with the manager, or from a mistake the employee may or may not have made.

I found it was extremely important to network and meet key managers in your company or business unit. Managers that knew my employees usually supported my recommendations.

Questions

1. What do you think are some of the things you can do to get a promotion? Is working hard the only way to get promoted or should you be vocal?

2. What are some of the things you can do to get more compensation?

3. Why would you want to plan for interactions with your manager?

4. Why would you want to plan for interactions with your manager's peers?

5. Why would you want to plan for interactions with your employees?

6. Why would you want to praise in public but give critical feedback in private to an employee or even a manager?

7. What are some examples when you were negotiating with your employer or even parents, both successful or unsuccessful? What do you ask for and why? What would you do differently?

14
Final Comments

You need to find your own style of negotiation. Follow the planning process and you will achieve better outcomes. The more prepared you are, the more comfortable you will be negotiating.

Read and understand the negotiating rules for each stage of negotiation. Pick two or three key tactics you think you can master. Practice your negotiation skills whenever you can. Offers are generally meant to be aggressive. Being aggressive will help you get concessions and better outcomes from the other party. Do not take offense to an offer, accept it as a gift, and then use it to negotiate a better deal.

Make your negotiations fun and you will be happier. Of course, there will be tense moments in any negotiation. I am constantly cracking jokes during negotiations. It lightens the mood.

Lastly, if everyone must get what they want, then no one gets anything except the most powerful. Hence, negotiations are necessary to living and life.

The Negotiation Process

1. Assess the opportunity (Chapter 3).

2. Develop a team and organization structure (Chapter 4).

3. Gather information (Chapter 5).

4. Develop negotiation positions and strategies (Chapter 6).

5. Negotiate externally (Chapter 7).

6. Close and Plan the transition (Chapter 8).

Negotiation Planning Rules

1. Always do your homework.
2. There is a correlation between aspiration level and outcome. If you do not ask for it, chances are you will not get it.
3. Determine your authority to negotiate.
4. Understand the authority of your counterparty
5. Cap liabilities and avoid tax indemnities, when possible.
6. Focus on underlying interests of your counterparty, not just contract positions.
7. Do not open with your bottom line on key issues.
8. Understand your counterparty's culture.
9. Find out and manage all deadlines.
10. Always have a mitigation plan for potential risks.
11. Find out as much as you can about your counterparty.

Negotiation Interaction Rules

1. There is only one Lead Negotiator on your side of the table.
2. Have pre-meetings with your team, agree on the agenda with your counterparty, and debrief the team after each negotiation.
3. Quid Pro Quo - seek information when giving information and a tradeoff for every concession.
4. Meet face to face; avoid email and telephone negotiations.
5. Question, question, question – both for clarification and information.
6. If you cannot be truthful, it is best not to say it. Be ethical.
7. Keep your negotiating team small and manage SMEs and executives.
8. Focus on the issues, not the personality.
9. Place risk on the party best able to control the risk or get paid to accept the risk.

10. Never immediately accept the other side's opening offer (and be careful changing a previously agreed-to clause).

11. Do not negotiate against yourself.

12. Trust by verifying.

13. Everything is negotiable.

14. Always have a plan for every interaction with your counterparty.

Key Negotiation Tactics

1. Set anchors.

2. Crunch.

3. Use silence as a weapon.

4. Practice patience and persistence.

5. Understand biases.

6. Use power.

7. Create and maintain competition.

8. Focus on and create small wins early for both parties.

9. Group issues at the end of the negotiation to suggest final solutions on all key issues to close the deal.

10. Leverage the power of loss aversion (group their losses).

11. Understand what non-verbal communications are telling you.

12. Avoid making a concession larger than the one preceding it on any issue

Negotiation Truisms

1. The moment of the opening offer is generally the most important and most stressful in the entire negotiation.

2. Stress levels change behaviors.

3. It is better to negotiate an issue when you have leverage.

4. For complicated business deals, you "need" a great, highly skilled lawyer and negotiator.

5. Your job as negotiator of a long-term contract is to get the best, most profitable, legal deal while letting the counter-party make "some" money.

6. If there is no zone of agreement on a key issue, then there is no deal.

Questions

1. What behaviors do you plan to change after reading this book? Why?

2. What tactics do you see yourself using in business or in life? Why?

3. What negotiation tactic did you find most important to yourself? Why?

4. What negotiation tactic did you find least valuable to yourself? Why?

5. What tactics have you used and what was the situation?

6. Give examples of negotiations you have been in where tactics were used. Explain in each negotiation what tactics were used and how they afected the outcome.

Appendix

Negotiation Alignment Framing Tool

Note: The tables below list the items that you will need to complete a negotiation frame; however, you are likely to need more room than the following pages provide. I recommend that you download our Excel® framing workbook file from http://www.decisions-books.com, as this will provide much more space for the items in your frame.

Negotiation Question	Problem, Risk, or Opportunity?
(High level statement of *what* we are negotiating and *why* we are negotiating.)	*What* are we trying to accomplish?
	Why are we trying to do this?

Boundary Conditions	
What are we negotiating (IN the frame)?	What are we *not* negotiating (OUT of the frame)?
ON the frame (unclear whether we should negotiate issue or not)?	

SWOT - Strengths, Weaknesses, Opportunities, and Threats (Internal and External)	
Strengths	Weaknesses
Opportunities	Threats

Negotiation Alignment Framing Tool (page 2)

Stakeholder Analysis (impacted entities)		
Name	Supporter or Detractor?	Communication Plan

Issue Raising: Objectives, decisions, risks and uncertainties, facts, assumptions, value drivers, and action items.

Issue	Category	Affected Party

Objectives Hierarchy
Fundamental Objective:
Supporting Objectives:
Means Objectives:

Decision Timeline
Past Decisions (givens):
Decisions that Must be Addressed Now:
Decisions that Can be Postponed:

Position Table

Issue	YOU	COUNTERPARTY	Notes
YOU Underlying Interests (drivers) Power / Ability to Influence		COUNTERPARTY Underlying Interests (drivers) Power / Ability to Influence	
Issue	1. Most Desired Outcome(s) 2. Bottom Line 3. Opening Position 4. BATNA		Notes

Biases that Affect Negotiations[15]

Name	Description
Ambiguity effect	The tendency to avoid options for which missing information makes the probability seem "unknown."
Anchoring	The tendency to rely too heavily, or "anchor," on one trait or piece of information when making decisions.
Bandwagon effect	The tendency to do (or believe) things because many other people do (or believe) the same. Related to groupthink and herd behavior.
Belief bias	An effect where someone's evaluation of the logical strength of an argument is biased by the believability of the conclusion.
Bias blind spot	The tendency to see oneself as less biased than other people, or to be able to identify more cognitive biases in others than in oneself.
Confirmation bias	The tendency to search for, interpret, focus on, and remember information in a way that confirms one's preconceptions.
Conservatism or regressive bias	A certain state of mind wherein high values and high likelihoods are overestimated while low values and low likelihoods are underestimated.
Conservatism	The tendency to insufficiently revise one's belief when presented with new evidence.
Endowment effect	The fact that people often demand much more to give up an object than they would be willing to pay to acquire it.
Experimenter's or expectation bias	The tendency for experimenters to believe, certify, and publish data that agree with their expectations for the outcome of an experiment, and to disbelieve, discard, or downgrade the corresponding weightings for data that appear to conflict with those expectations.

---

15 Wikipedia.com has a very good detailed description of the biases noted in this table.

Name	Description
Framing effect	Drawing different conclusions from the same information, depending on how or by whom that information is presented.
Gambler's fallacy	The tendency to think that future probabilities are altered by past events, when in reality they are unchanged. Results from an erroneous conceptualization of the law of large numbers. For example, "I have flipped heads with this coin five times consecutively, so the chance of tails coming out on the sixth flip is much greater than heads."
Illusion of validity	Belief that further acquired information generates additional relevant data for predictions, even when it evidently does not.
Information bias	The tendency to seek information even when it cannot affect action.
Irrational escalation	The phenomenon where people justify increased investment in a decision, based on the cumulative prior investment, despite new evidence suggesting that the decision was probably wrong. Also known as the sunk cost fallacy.
Loss aversion	"...the disutility of giving up an object is greater than the utility associated with acquiring it." (See also Sunk cost effects and endowment effect.).
Negativity bias	Psychological phenomenon by which humans have a greater recall of unpleasant memories compared to positive memories.
Neglect of probability	The tendency to completely disregard probability when making a decision under uncertainty.
Overconfidence effect	Excessive confidence in one's own answers to questions. For example, for certain types of questions, answers that people rate as "99% certain" turn out to be wrong 40% of the time.
Planning fallacy	The tendency to underestimate task completion times.
Status quo bias	The tendency to like things to stay relatively the same (see also loss aversion, endowment effect, and system justification).

About the Author

Craig McKnight is the semi-retired owner of QD Negotiations, LLC with focus on negotiation training and preparation. Craig spent the last ten years of his career developing negotiation training and then teaching negotiation and decision process courses throughout Chevron worldwide.

He retired in 2016 as Manager of Decision & Economic Analysis for the Deepwater Exploration & Projects and Gulf of Mexico business units for Chevron. Headquartered in Houston, Craig was responsible for decision quality and economic analysis for oil and gas exploration, appraisal, capital, and technology projects in the business units.

Craig received an accounting degree from Sam Houston State University in 1980. He received his Doctorate in Jurisprudence from South Texas College of Law Houston in 1992. He became a CPA in 1985 and a lawyer in 1992.

He began his career at Texaco in 1980 as an accountant. He has held a variety of roles in Texaco and Chevron, including capital stewardship champion, International gas regional commercial manager – Latin America, International gas decision analysis team leader, planning manager, and executive staff. He has also held positions outside Chevron as an investment banker, lawyer, and tax specialist.

At the writing of this book, Craig is a member of the Society of Decision Professionals, the Decision Analysis Affinity Group, and a board member of the Houston chapter of the Society of Decision Professionals.

Craig and Ginger McKnight

Index

Other Books from Probabilistic Publishing

Introduction to Decision Analysis 3rd Edition, by David C. Skinner

Subtitle: A Practitioner's Guide to Improving Decision Quality

Mr. Skinner originally wrote Introduction to Decision Analysis as a handbook and guide for the Decision Analysis (DA) practitioner in 1995. The 2nd Edition was published in 1999 and quickly became an essential reference for industry as well as a graduate-level textbook for decision analysis courses at many universities. Feedback from students, practitioners, and professors was incorporated into the 3rd Edition, which was released in 2009.

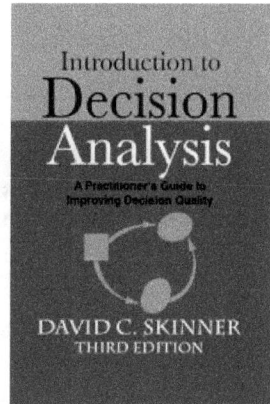

Introduction to Decision Analysis is recommended for DA consultants, corporate DA practitioners, managers and technical professionals who are responsible for making effective decisions, and for MBA or other graduate-level students.

David draws heavily on his 25 years of experience in consulting, teaching, and starting new businesses. The Editor, Paul Wicker, is also an experienced DA consultant and trainer with an extensive background in oil, gas, and chemicals.

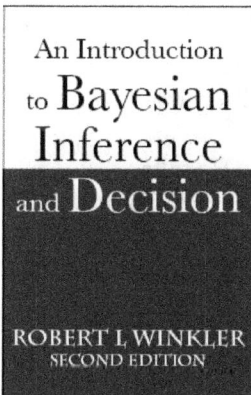

Introduction to Bayesian Inference and Decision

2nd Edition, by Robert Winkler

The basic concepts of Bayesian inference and decision have not really changed since the first edition of this book was published in 1972. Even so, Bayesian inference and decision has been a very fertile and rapidly growing field, both in terms of theoretical/methodological research and in terms of real-world applications.

This book gives a foundation in the concepts, enables readers to understand the results of analyses in Bayesian inference and decision, provides tools to model real-world problems and carry out basic analyses, and prepares readers for further explorations in Bayesian inference and decision. In the second edition, material has been added on some topics, examples and exercises have been updated, and perspectives have been added to each chapter and the end of the book to indicate how the field has changed and to give some new references.

Why Can't You Just Give Me The Number? 2nd Edition, by Patrick Leach

Subtitle: An Executive's Guide to Using Probabilistic Thinking to Manage Risk and to Make Better Decisions

Patrick Leach draws on his extensive consulting and teaching experience to present a compelling, insightful, and understandable case for using probabilistic analysis as part of everyday business decision making. Practical examples and case studies are clearly presented.

Mr. Leach is an experienced conference speaker, business trainer, and consultant. He makes a clear, concise case for appropriate implementation of probabilistic analysis. Rather than get bogged down with equations and complexity, he shares his insight and the benefits of his experience (and some key research by others) in a way that is readable, useful, and memorable.

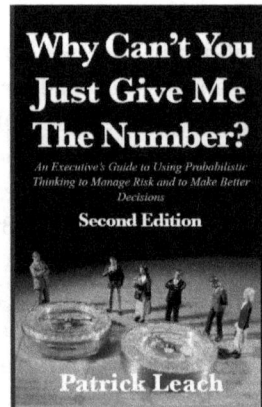

Game Theory for Business by Paul Papayoanou

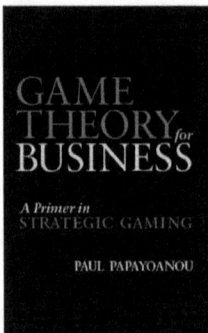

Subtitle: A Primer in Strategic Gaming

Dr. Papayoanou has written a clear, complete, interesting, and concise guide to applying game theory in business situations. He takes a uniquely practical yet rigorous approach with both the book and his consulting projects. As a DA practitioner and having spent extensive time with Dr. Papayoanou's text, my conclusion is that DA is to checkers as Strategic Gaming is to chess: it represents a higher, more difficult, yet more powerful level of thinking.

Creating a Culture of Profitability by Rob and Aviva Kleinbaum

Subtitle: A Revolutionary Model for Managing Culture

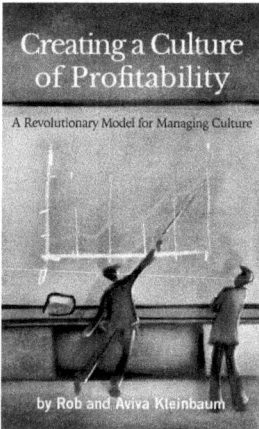

Improving culture in business has been a "soft" and subjective topic – until now. Rob and Aviva Kleinbaum have used Lawrence Harrison's 30-year study of successful cultures as the foundation for a powerful and logical framework for analyzing and improving business culture.

Building on this research and integrating the work of others, the Kleinbaums have developed a conceptual model that is useful, based on data, and testable against experience. There are symptoms and metrics for the cultural ills that reveal problems before they become overpowering. They suggest reasonable and doable treatment plans that attack the symptoms and root causes. There is a workable plan for getting started and integrating cultural management into the existing organization, without adding bureaucracy or overhead. Culture matters. Everyone knows that. But now something can be done about it.

Project Risk Quantification by John K. Hollmann

Subtitle: A Practitioner's Guide to Realistic Cost and Schedule Risk Management

Project Risk Quantification presents the most practical, realistic, and integrated approach to project cost and schedule risk quantification that is available today! It offers proven, empirically-valid methods and tools applicable to projects of all types and at all decision gates. The text is written for both the manager and the risk analysis practitioner. It will bring reliable accuracy and contingency determination to your capital project organization.

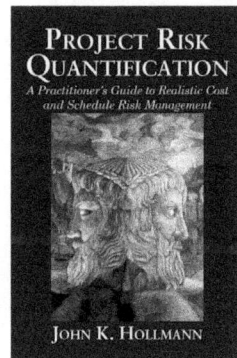

Problem, Risk, and Opportunity Enterprise Management by Brian W. Hagen

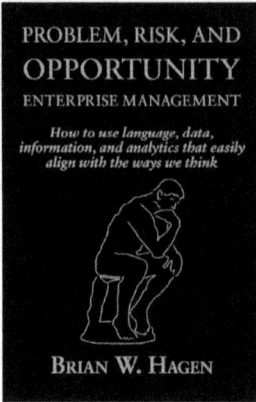

PROBLEM, RISK, AND
OPPORTUNITY
ENTERPRISE MANAGEMENT

How to use language, data, information, and analytics that easily align with the ways we think

BRIAN W. HAGEN

Subtitle: How to use language, data, information, and analytics that easily align with the ways we think.

Through decades of consulting practice, Dr. Hagen has tailored a decision-making process to correspond with the way that our brains actually function. This comprehensive book shares his methodology and the basis for it. He presents powerful insights and distinctions that are not found elsewhere.

"Finally, someone has developed the missing link—a sound methodology that more clearly and directly ties risk management to decision making. Brian Hagen argues successfully that enterprise risk management is primarily a decision-making process that must be integrated into a coherent, repeatable, enterprise-wide method to manage your portfolio of decisions across problems, risks and opportunities. He includes compelling arguments and robust examples that demonstrate how to quantify the alternatives, thereby improving business and financial decisions."

–Jay R. Taylor, former General Director,
Strategic Risk Management, GM

www.ingramcontent.com/pod-product-compliance
Lightning Source LLC
Chambersburg PA
CBHW061315220326
41599CB00026B/4891